A Father to Many

Esteban Uriburu

A Father to Many

The Life and Work

of

Father Joseph Kentenich

Translation: M. Cole
Uriburu, Esteban J.:
Sie nennen ihn Vater: Leben und Wirken des Pater Kentenich/
Esteban Uriburu – a translation of the Spanish text by Antonio
Bracht; edited by Hans-Werner Unkel.
Spanish edition: Un profeta de María, Biografía del Padre José
Kentenich/P. Esteban J. Uriburu. Editorial Clarentiana, Buenos
Aires 1981

Esteban José Uriburu was born in Buenos Aires on 9 May 1937. He completed his secondary education at the Jesuit College in Buenos Aires and obtained his Bachelor's degree in 1953. In 1954 he entered the Faculty of Law at Buenos Aires and graduated as a lawyer in 1960. In the same year he set out on the way to the priesthood, carrying out his studies in Chile, Brazil and Germany. He was ordained a priest as a member of the community of the Schoenstatt Fathers in March 1971, and spent the next three years (1971–73) working in a parish in Santiago, Chile. From 1974 he worked in Buenos Aires serving the Schoenstatt Movement. In 1977 he took over responsibility for the Pilgrims' Movement to the shrine of our Lady of Schoenstatt at Florencio Varela. From 1978–1980 he collaborated in the preparations for the National Marian Congress held in 1980. He has published a number of works in Spanish: Testimonios sobre el Padre Kentenich (1972); Mario Hiriart (1973); Barbara Kast (1974); Un Profeta (1975). This work is the translation of his last book, which has also been translated into German.

CONTENTS

1. FOREWORD

It takes time to appreciate a gift correctly. You need the perspective of time if you are to grasp its depth and importance. This has been my experience with regard to Fr Kentenich. I consider that being allowed to get to know him and follow in his footsteps is a great gift. I shall never forget the sunny morning of 2 April 1965 when I saw him for the first time. He was just coming out of the little shrine of the Mother Thrice Admirable of Schoenstatt, which is situated behind the parish church of Holy Cross, Milwaukee, USA. He was quiet and recollected as he walked over the snow-covered pathway to the presbytery, his white beard lit up by the rising sun. The moment when I met him for the first time in the sacristy remains imprinted indelibly on my memory. The light in his eyes, the penetration of his look, his fatherly kindness and his human warmth all impressed me deeply. Although I had never seen him before, I was immediately able to trust him unreservedly and completely.

Fifteen years have passed since that first meeting in Milwaukee. In the normal course of events memories lose their clarity and freshness as time goes by, almost as though a fine layer of dust gradually settles on them. This is not the case with my memories of Fr Kentenich. Instead of slowly fading, his personality appears with ever growing clarity before me. It has become increasingly demarcated and timely. I have to admit that it exercises as much attraction on me today as it did on the day I first met him; indeed, this has even increased. The years that have passed and the experiences I have gathered have helped me to a better understanding of many things he said at that time. And so I have begun to want to write about his life. It is not the first time that such an attempt has been made. Fr Engelbert Monnerjahn has written a comprehensive biography based on thorough and extensive study of the documentary sources (*Father Joseph Kentenich, a Life for the Church*, Vallendar, Schönstatt, Patris-Verlag 1975). No one who wants to study the life of this great priest can afford to pass over this work. However, if I see things rightly, what is needed is a shorter, simpler work that will make his life accessible to a wider circle of readers.

Apart from one or two short trips I stayed in Milwaukee for five and a half years. Every morning I took part in the Holy Mass he celebrated punctually at 5.50 a.m. in the shrine. On Sundays I attended the 10 o'clock Holy Mass in the crypt of St Michael's Church which he offered for the German-speaking community, of which he was the chaplain. Now and again I served as interpreter (from Spanish into English and vice versa), and for one reason or another I had various opportunities to be close to him. It even happened that on many occasions we were able to chat with each other personally.

When Father Kentenich was called to Rome in September 1965 after spending thirteen years in exile in Milwaukee, I had the chance to meet him again at the John F. Kennedy Airport. That was an unforgettable afternoon on 16 September 1965. I saw him once again in March the following year on Mount Schoenstatt, when we had supper together in the "Schulungsheim" (Training Centre).

On entering the newly-founded community of the

Schoenstatt Fathers, I undertook my theology studies at Münster, Westphalia, from 1966 – 1970. In this way it was possible to be in contact with him in the last years of his priestly activity in Schoenstatt. Without doubt it was much more difficult to get to see him in those days than when he was in Milwaukee. However, I did have the opportunity to talk to him personally on a couple of occasions.

I took part in the large congresses he conducted in Schoenstatt in October and December of 1966 and 1967. Father Kentenich came to Münster, where we were studying (Dettenianum College, Schmeddingsstrasse 50), from 22 – 25 August 1967 to conduct our retreat. Altogether there were about forty students who took part, and apart from the three conferences he gave us daily, he dedicated half an hour of his time to each one personally. It was in Münster, too, that we heard the news of his sudden death on Sunday, 15 September 1968. All the students travelled to Schoenstatt on the 19th and participated in his Requiem and burial on the following day.

My aim is to highlight, from a flood of reports and an abundance of events, those features of his personality that will be of importance to us today and tomorrow. His life, which covers the years between 1885 and 1968, spans a period in time in which an unprecedented change of historical proportions has taken place. Geoffrey Barraclough, Toynbee's successor to the Chair of History at the Stephenson Research Institute at London University, has described this period of time as the line of demarcation between two eras, as the turning-point marking the end of one and the start of a new epoch.

In the almost sixty years of his active and fruitful priestly service (1910-1968) we find two world wars, the Russian and the Chinese Revolutions. Science and technology have developed with enormous speed. Great Popes such as Leo XIII, Pius X, Pius XI, Pius XII, John XXIII and Paul VI were Fr Kentenich's contemporaries. He was staying in Rome during the last session of the Second Vatican Council. He experienced and suffered the murderous cruelties of the concentration camp at Dachau (1942-1945). With prophetic vision he grasped what was ultimately at stake in the present-day historical developments. With reference to them he wrote from his prison cell in Coblenz, "On the horizon, gradually becoming clearly recognizable, the great structural lines of a new world order are coming into view; and an old world is in flames..." Neither the experience of two world wars, nor the observation of physical, moral and intellectual catastrophes, which characterise our epoch, made him a prophet of pessimism and doom. Through faith and hope he could foresee that they were leading to a new beginning, they were the painful birthpangs of a new world being brought into existence by God. "It must be a most wonderful world that he is causing to arise out of these violent death throes, it must be a wonderful order that he wants to re-create out of catastrophes and ruins."

It was given to him to see the greatness of Mary's mission in the gigantic dimensions of this dramatic process of transformation. She should give birth to Christ anew for this new world that is in the process of coming into existence. He was meant to be the instrument through which Mary wanted to bind herself to the shrine at

Schoenstatt, so that she might reveal her glories from there, particularly as the educator of a new, free and childlike person. His personal relationship to Mary proceeded from a very profound experience that reaches back into his childhood. (Yet Mary never appeared to him, nor did he have any private revelations.) During the crisis which marked his youth and his studies for the priesthood, and which was so extreme that it brought him to the brink of mental breakdown, because he could not reconcile the double dimension of reality, the human and the divine, in theory or practice, he discovered that Mary is the person in whom nature and grace are brought to perfect harmony. She is the "balance of the world". He later stated that during the struggles of his youth he had suffered through that disease which at bottom afflicts the West today. Together with the malady he was allowed to experience the remedy. That is why he did not hesitate to confess, "Mary is the soul of my soul". He considered it his mission to proclaim the mystery of Mary to the world, "with the specific mission she has been given to carry out from her Schoenstatt Shrine for the present era". Like every prophet, he was not understood by many, and others even despised him. Nevertheless, in the almost sixty years of his priesthood he was unshakable in upholding his fundamental convictions. He considered it a great honour to be allowed to fight and suffer for them, so that Mary's mission and position in the order of salvation might be acknowledged in his home country, Germany, and throughout the Church and world.

This book can naturally not do justice to Fr Kentenich's many-faceted personality. When a person has been formed into a particularly successful image of Christ, God makes his presence and his features known in a vital way to man. We are then faced with a divine mystery, with something sublime and holy. May this book be of assistance in bringing closer to modern man, who sadly lacks really great examples, a life which can be a guiding light and which can awaken courageous hope.

Forward to the English Edition

"Our hearts belong to all people, to all nations, whatever their name or their history." Father Joseph Kentenich spoke these words on 8 December 1944 in the concentration camp at Dachau. They were the expression not only of his inmost attitude, but also of his life.

It is a reason to rejoice to know of the publication of the English edition of this brief biography of the founder of the Schoenstatt Family. I am thinking of all those English-speaking people spread throughout the world – in South Africa, Great Britain, the United States or Australia – who have entered into a convenant of love in the shrine. I am also thinking of all those who will be enriched by contact with the priestly personality of Father Kentenich, finding in him valid answers to present-day challenges, and a father and intercessor in heaven.

I sincerely thank the Schoenstatt Sisters of Mary in South Africa for their work of translation and editing. May the work they have done receive an abundant reward.

1/5/83   FATHER ESTEBAN J. URIBURU

14

2. CHILDHOOD AND YOUTH

Although the amazing progress in science and technology has given man an unprecedented power over nature, life continues to be surrounded by mystery, and will forever remain so. Sometimes people with great destinies are born into socially important families, but it has also happened that great men have risen from insignificant backgrounds. (''How often in world history has not the small and insignificant been the source of the great and greatest'' – Fr Kentenich.) This apparent contradiction is, however, a constant with which we are confronted again and again in world and salvation history. St. Paul explained it to the Corinthians in the following words: ''No, it was to shame the wise that God chose what is foolish by human reckoning, and to shame what is strong that he chose what is weak by human reckoning; those whom the world thinks common and contemptible are the ones that God has chosen – those who are nothing at all to show up those who are everything. The human race has nothing to boast about to God'' (1 Cor. 1: 27 – 29). Many who visit Schoenstatt for the first time say in surprise, ''I never imagined that it was so big; I thought there was a small shrine in the valley, a pilgrims' square, some houses, and nothing else''. The Adoration Church on Mount Schoenstatt, which is dedicated to the Blessed Trinity, and in which Fr Kentenich died and is buried, awakens a sense of peace, security and eternity in pilgrims. However, this great work has its origin in what is very small – a farming village called Gymnich, near Cologne.

Although it is an insignificant little village, one of the hundreds strewn across the Rhineland, Gymnich has a long history. A Roman legion stationed in the vicinity, the "Legio Gemina", gave the village its name: Geminiacum. Later this became "Gemmenich", and finally "Gymnich". The visitor's gaze is involuntarily drawn from the typical houses of the village to two large buildings opposite them – the parish church with its onion-shaped dome, which is dedicated to St Kunibert (Bishop of Cologne, died 633), and the castle belonging to the Lords of Gymnich dating back to the 16th century. It is surrounded by a beautiful park that is enclosed by a moat. (In winter, when the water was frozen, young Joseph and his friends enjoyed playing on the ice.) Important events in European history took place near Gymnich. Not far away, at Zülpich, the decisive battle for the Christianisation of Europe took place. King Clovis of the Franks was the victor and thereupon allowed St Remigius to baptise him. This was the beginning of the conversion of the "barbarians". However, it was another event that left an even greater mark on the village. This took place in the life of Arnold von Gymnich, a knight living in the 13th century. Tradition reports that Arnold I took part in the Fifth Crusade, and in 1218 found himself at the Nile Delta. As the Crusaders began to advance on Cairo, the Musulmans opened the Nile dams and flooded the valley through which they were marching. Arnold was one of the few men who was able to save himself out of the morass. When he tried to flee, his horse was caught in the swamp and began to sink. At the last moment he asked God to save him, and promised that a procession would take place every year in his village in remembrance of God's intervention. We are told that a bird suddenly let out a cry which frightened the horse to such an extent that it shied violently and with that found firm ground under its feet. Arnold had been saved. Since then, down through the centuries, the people of Gymnich have ridden in procession through the village on the feast of the Ascension. (At the beginning of May 1978, the Russian Premier Breshnev was staying in Gymnich Castle during an official visit to Germany, since this castle has been restored by the Bonn Government as a residence for high-ranking guests. Since this visit coincided with the feast of the Ascension, and hence also with the procession, the government asked the town council to postpone the procession. The people protested, stating that even under the Nazi regime the procession had taken place on Ascension Day. The result was that even in that year the procession on horseback took place on the usual day, and Breshnev entered the castle by a side entrance.)

This was the region in which a small group of children was growing up towards the end of the last century. Among them was a lively, intelligent boy with a clear and penetrating look: Joseph Kentenich. He was born on 18 November 1885, and he was baptised the following day in the parish church of St Kunibert, receiving the names Peter Joseph. He was always called Joseph. His father, Matthias Joseph, came from the neighbouring village of Eggersheim and was engaged in farming. As a young man he fought in the 1870/71 war as a lancer in one of the crack German cavalry regiments. It is related that he had an unusually strong will. When he rode home at night, he never allowed his tiredness to show, but sat erect in the saddle. Joseph's mother Katharina, came from a good farming family. She was a kind woman of simple beauty, the youngest of a large family. She was deeply religious and had a special love for Mary, the Mother of God. She dedicated her child to our Lady even before his birth.

Little Joseph grew up in the home of his mother's parents, because adverse circumstances forced her to go out to work in order to provide for her child. He was like every other child, and yet he was also quite different. So it was that he grew up with a growing sense of loneliness, although no one else was aware of it.

A number of anecdotes have been handed down to us from his childhood. He was twice in danger of death. One day a cow on the rampage tossed the basket with the infant, sending it sailing through the air in the direction of a brook. Except for a tremendous fright (which was to be expected), there were no other consequences. On another occasion, when he was three, he was playing hide-and-seek with his cousin, Henriette, and another girl in the neighbour's house and fell into a well. His life was saved thanks to his cousin's alarmed cries for help and the prompt action of his grandfather, who was having a chat with the owner of the house not far away. When Joseph was hauled out of the well he was unconscious. A nurse laid him on a bed and tried all sorts of things to induce him to react. ''Joseph will soon be well again,'' she said loudly, ''then he can go to the Kindergarten and will get a pretty picture.'' The child moved, opened his eyes and said firmly, ''I won't go to the Kindergarten and I don't want a picture!'' And he lost consciousness again. It was a typical reaction. It showed his innate dislike of any form of outward coercion. His cousin relates another incident. At that time school children still used slates. Joseph, who was seven or eight at the time, had finished his homework. While she was cleaning the edge of the slate, his cousin rubbed out a word by mistake. When Joseph presented his slate to the teacher the following day, he was asked who had done his homework for him. "I did it myself," Joseph replied. "No, someone helped you," the teacher said. "No, no one helped me," answered the boy. "You are lying," the teacher insisted. "That is not your writing." And he showed the boy his slate. The child was quite at a loss and did not know what to say. It was true, someone else had written on his slate. His cousin, who was in the same class, watched this without saying a word. As they left school she told him, "I rubbed out the word and then wrote it over again. But I didn't dare to tell you or the teacher." The boy looked at her seriously, and no more was said.

When he was six his mother took him with her to Strassburg, which was then part of Germany. Her brother, Peter Joseph, whose wife had died, had asked her to come and look after his house and three children. It was there that the boy came to know the prayer:

"Help us, Mary, e'er we fall,
Mother of Mercy, to you we call.
You are powerful, you can save us
from all needs and threatening dangers.
When all human help has failed us,
yours will never be denied us.
You cannot withstand the prayers
of your children in their fears."

After her brother had married again, Katharina returned to Gymnich with little Joseph, who continued his schooling. He enjoyed learning and found it exceptionally easy. However, he did not like going to school. He instinctively rejected the current teaching methods which required learning by heart, sitting still without being allowed to move, the Prussian discipline. This system ran completely contrary to his nature and his personal disposition. It was only as time went by that this revealed typical features of his personality – his love for freedom, or to be more precise, his love for the free personality. Even at that time he felt a stranger in the world around him, although he was not yet consciously aware of it. He was later to say, ''As far back as I can remember, I saw clearly and took it for granted that I had to create the new man who is not dependent on outward slogans, who can decide for himself, and who goes his way free of outward drill. That was simply a part of my personality, it just developed in me.''

On 12 April 1894 Katharina brought her son to the St Vincent Orphanage at Oberhausen. Why did she go there? Because she could not have her child with her all the time, she had been advised by her confessor, Fr August Savels, to act in this way. Savels had founded the orphanage, and at that time he was parish priest of ''The Apostles'', Cologne. There were about two hundred children in the orphanage at the time. The place was clean and tidy despite being overcrowded. The children only wore shoes on Sundays and feastdays. During the week they were barefooted. There was meat only on Sundays. The 12 April was a hard day for his mother. Even though she knew that her son was in good hands, she still had to part from him. Before she returned to Cologne, she went to the house chapel with the boy and kneeling with simple faith in front of a statue of Mary, she entrusted the education of her son to the Mother of God. She took her golden cross and chain, the gift of her godmother at her First Communion, and hung it around our Lady's neck as a visible sign of this consecration. The child observed everything. It is possible that his mother acted without saying a word, but her gesture must have made a deep impression on little Joseph's heart. Something also took place between him and our Lady, because he was later to describe the 12 April 1894 as one of the decisive moments in his relationship to the Mother of God and in his life as such. In the address he gave at the silver jubilee of his ordination he said, ''My education has simply been the work of the Mother of God without any deeper human influence. She has personally formed and moulded me since my ninth year.''

Life in the orphanage was very hard because it was ruled with iron discipline. Joseph felt his longing for freedom so severely suppressed that he tried to run away on two occasions. (We are told that each time the police recognized the school uniform of the house and brought him back.) On the whole he was a good and religious child. A sister recalls the following incident: The children slept on the top floor. At a certain time they had to keep silence. On one occasion Joseph was caught talking. For punishment he was sent to the bathroom for ten minutes. The boy obeyed. However, after the ten minutes were up he did not return, so the sister became uneasy and went to look for him. On opening the door she found Joseph kneeling there steeped in prayer.

In 1897, when he was eleven, he received two sacraments. On Low Sunday he received his First Holy Communion (on this day he told his mother that he wanted to be a priest), and on 24 September he was confirmed. He spent five years in all at the orphanage. An outsider might not consider this a long time, but it was very long for someone who suffered under this form of education. His childhood was definitely not a happy one. And yet this child was one day as a priest to make hundreds, even thousands, of people happy in the almost sixty years of his active ministry.

He was not quite fourteen when Fr Savels accompanied him to Ehrenbreitstein near Coblenz on 23 September 1899, so that he might enter the Pallottine Minor Seminary there. This house had been in service since 1893 to train future missionaries for the Cameroons, at that time a German colony in Africa.

Joseph was a few days late in joining the winter semester 1899/1900, but he had no difficulty in catching up with the rhythm of studies. He was a hard-working and hard-striving student. He soon made good contact with his teacher, Fr. Johann Mayer, and sent him a 55-line poem for Christmas that year. It was entitled, "The Gift of the Wise", and was accompanied by the following dedication: "Herewith I wish to express my sincere gratitude for all the kindness you have shown me in the short time I have been here, and particularly for the consolation you have given me in my circumstances. May God reward you. I shall remember you daily in my prayers, that you may be given the necessary strength to lead us correctly and keep us on the good path, and that the heavy burden of your duties may be lightened. Once again thanking you for everything, I remain your grateful scholar and pupil, Joseph Kentenich." Gratitude, the mark of all noble-minded souls, was to accompany him throughout his life. He was grateful to the living God and to man. In all probability he was already suffering from poor health at this time. This could be a reason why his mother opposed his wish to become a priest. It seems that a difficulty in his relationship to his mother had cropped up in this first year at Ehrenbreitstein. This is indicated by a poem he wrote before Easter 1900. It is entitled, "The Power of Love".

O Lord, I commend myself to you!
Let your heart soften, I beg of you!
... Direct my mother's mind and heart,
– I would not like to cause her pain –
that she may let me do my will.
His tears he can no longer still.
A priest is what I would become
my thoughts have grown most burdensome.
Oh God, prevent what I so dread,
I would far sooner lie there dead,
than not to answer to your call
and in the priesthood give my all.
For this you made me, oh my God,
I hear you calling, you are my Lord.
I would obey you, though I know
'tis hard to love you as is due.
So I shall struggle from today
my mother's problems to allay.
Give me the grace to do this, Lord,
then shall my life give praise to God.

Five years later, in the 1904 semester, Joseph completed his classical studies. He was almost nineteen. As that period in his life came to a close and a new life opened before him, the soul of the young student was filled with sadness for what was passing, as well as hope for what was starting. This is revealed in a letter he wrote to Fr Mayer during his holidays. ''I like to think back on the past years. I am overcome by a feeling of sadness when I recall that I have, or that I must now break off my classical studies. It was a lovely time! Could it ever return one day? Perhaps I shall enjoy my higher studies as much. At any rate I hope so.''

3. THE WAY TO THE PRIESTHOOD

The radical decision to lead a celibate and virginal life is a process that goes far beyond merely human reckoning; it is always impressive. The less sense an epoch has for God and for the reality of the supernatural world, the more difficult it becomes for it to grasp the value and the importance of such decisions. Nevertheless, whether the world possesses an understanding for it or not, the Lord calls young people to leave everything and follow him. "Whoever has left father or mother for my sake" (cf Mark 10: 29). Of course, there are different ways that lead to the priesthood. In the normal course of events a vocation matures slowly. Some experience their calling in their childhood, others discover it later, others again suddenly become aware of God's call. There is something common to all these ways: we are not in the first place concerned with a human choice, but with a divine election. "You did not choose me, no, I chose you" (John 15: 16). Man's part – often in the darkness of faith and contrary to all his feelings – is to answer this soft, this urging, this insistent call that yet respects man's free decision. It is a call that makes demands, but which at the same time also offers the necessary graces.

Joseph Kentenich had always possessed a strong inclination towards God, towards the absolute and eternal. This was not the fruit of his own efforts, it was simply his personal structure. The result was that merely natural things held very little attraction for him.

With regard to women, he had never known a friendship with a girl. It never entered his mind that he could marry. We may not suppose that this was because he undervalued women or womanhood. On the contrary, he was to exercise a profound influence on hundreds, even thousands, of women. God had chosen him. Yes, that was the simple fact – God had chosen him. However, until he had found the balance between the natural and the supernatural, between the human and the divine, his one-sided emphasis on the supernatural plunged him into a long and severe crisis.

He received the habit of the Pallottine Society on 24 September 1904, and his novitiate began in the beautifully situated medieval town of Limburg on the River Lahn. Around the year 910 Duke Konrad von Kurzbold donated a piece of land on which Duke Heinrich von Isenburg erected the present Cathedral of St George with its seven towers at the beginning of the 13th century. Teodorik, Bishop of Treves, consecrated it in 1235. The Pallottine Fathers had established themselves in this town after Fr Maximilian Kugelmann, the first superior in Germany, had completed the building of the new Mission House in 1898.

In what does the novitiate consist? The period of one or two years serves the work of personal formation. During this time the foundations for the religious life are laid. That is why the emphasis is not placed on study, but on the gradual introduction by stages into the life of the spirit. The novitiate is a time of recollection, silence and prayer, which should lead to deeper self-knowledge and the clarification of one's personal calling. One characteristic of the novitiate should be sound joy, even though trials and difficulties may not be lacking. A difficult period had started for Joseph Kentenich.

In a letter of 11.12.1916 he wrote, "From the time I entered the novitiate until my ordination, and even somewhat after that, I had constantly to cope with the most terrific struggles. There wasn't a trace of inner happiness and contentment." What was the reason? On the one hand, he was not understood by his spiritual director. This fact is painful enough when life is normal, but even more so in such an intense rhythm as is presented by life in the novitiate. It is natural that the young novice looked for inner support from the spiritual director. But he did not find it – either from him or from anyone else. This was the reason for the loneliness he had to suffer. "When I look back," he said at the silver jubilee of his ordination, "I may say that I know of no person who has exercised a deep influence on my development. Millions of people would have been broken if they had been thrown back on themselves as I was. I had to grow up completely alone in the depths of my soul."

However, he was not just suffering from loneliness. It was more. What was the crux of his difficulties? Outwardly Fr Kentenich was normal, he was just like all the others. But inwardly he was in ferment. He found himself in a crisis that threatened his very existence. He later described it in the following terms: "Because of the separation of my mind and my soul from what is earthly, from what is genuinely human, from temporal reality, the whole person was inwardly tortured and thrown to and fro by a total scepticism, by an exaggerated idealism, and by a one-sided supernaturalism." The young Kentenich believed that it was "total scepticism". But he asked himself the question, "Is there such a thing as truth? And if there is, how can we recognise it?" He sought God with his intellect, but could not find him in life. An "exaggerated idealism" – this showed in his relationship to others as a form of individualism, which made any genuinely human encounter impossible. Finally, a "one-sided supernaturalism", which prevented him from grasping the wholeness of reality, its double dimension of the human and the divine, and of experiencing their vital unity. At bottom he suffered in anticipation the intellectual problems to be found today in the West and in modern man. That is to say, the inability to grasp the mysterious, but real, interaction between earthly and eternal cities; the inability to create a vital synthesis between the human and the divine; to become aware of the relatedness between the creature and his Creator; in a word, to overcome the decisive separation between faith and daily life (cf Pastoral Constitution of the Church in the Modern World, No. 43, Second Vatican Council). Later Fr Kentenich spoke of a "disease germ" that had attacked the Western soul, of a "bacillus" that has to be done away with. He called it "mechanistic thinking".

We must pause here for a moment. What did Fr Kentenich mean when he spoke of "mechanistic thinking"? It is the opposite to "organic thinking", which is concerned with an all-comprising vision of reality, with a way of looking at things which is able to bring the visible and the invisible, the human and the divine, nature and grace, man and God together. "Mechanistic thinking" regards reality in an atomising, separating manner. It leads to a mentality that separates things that belong together, as well as life-processes from each other, it destroys what is living unity, tries to break up and analyse everything, and so inevitably leads us into a cul-de-sac. This mentality does not remain on the level of theory, it finds expression in the way we live and love. "That was my personal struggle in my youth," Fr Kentenich later admitted. "I had to fight through what is shaking the West today to its deepest roots." The crisis through which young Kentenich had to go did not remain on an intellectual level. It involved him wholly and even attacked his health. During the second year of his studies, his delicate state of health caused his superiors to consult the general council in Rome about admitting him to Profession for another year. Another student, who was two years ahead of him, remembers seeing him as a weak and sickly young man. He and another novice were given the special permission to withdraw from any gathering and lie down. (This was something Fr Kentenich disliked heartily.) The two usually did not take part in class outings. The others gave them a nickname – they belonged to the "Exceptions' Club".

He was so completely drawn into this crisis that he felt that he was on the verge of losing his mind. Since he was totally thrown back on himself and had no one to whom he could turn for help, he surrendered himself radically into our Lady's hands. He even wanted to accept the possibility of a complete mental breakdown. ("God had given me a clear mind, so I had to go through years of struggles in faith. What preserved the faith for me in all those years was a deep and simple love for Mary.") That was the start of his healing. He found his personal balance in the Mother of God; he saw in her how the human and the divine come together in a wonderful harmony.

"In her perfected nature," he wrote in 1939, "Mary is the classic point of intersection for nature and supernature, the unique embodiment of the harmonious combination of nature and grace". In his experience, Mary was Mother, Intercessor and Mediatrix. Even more, he grasped her importance for mankind as such. Mary gives us a sound way of thinking. That was his fundamental intuition which was to be confirmed again and again in everyday life. "Actually love for Mary always gives us this organic way of thinking." He realised the importance of our Lady herself in overcoming the anthropological crisis of our days, because she stands before us as the fully human, redeemed Woman in whom the human and the divine are wonderfully linked. This casts light on the importance of devotion to Mary, not only for the religious sphere, but also and above all for the anthropological. Pope Paul VI called our Lady the "miracle of true humanity", and in his encyclical letter, "Marialis Cultus", stressed the necessity of giving devotion to Mary an anthropological dimension.

The battles and suffering of these years of his novitiate and clerical studies were to give a decisive stamp to Fr Kentenich's personality as a priest. Throughout his life he was to be "the great devotee of the Mother of God", with whom he was "in love", as it were. In Mary he found not only the solution to his own existential needs, but also a key-figure in God's strategy to solve the present-day crisis of mankind. Despite a great deal of opposition and many difficulties, he was to proclaim her name and her mission courageously, and it was to be his constant concern to enkindle love and "burning enthusiasm for her personally in the widest possible circles''. Fr Michael Kolb, who was Rector of the House at the time, notes two incidents in his memoirs that reveal something of Novice Kentenich's deep relationship to the Mother of God. On 8 December 1904, on the fiftieth anniversary of the proclamation of the dogma of the Immaculate Conception, a commemorative act was held in the house. Among other items on the programme was a poem in honour of the Mother of God to be presented by young Kentenich. But when his turn came, he did not appear. What had happened? The Novice Master had cancelled it, because he did not think it advisable for such a recent novice to appear publicly. The Rector demanded that he should appear immediately. ''Since the situation demanded speedy action, I spoke authoritatively and required the Brother to come to the podium immediately. And that is what happened. The young Brother had to present his poem without any proper preparation. He did it with an enthusiasm and fire I have never witnessed in him again.'' The other event took place in May, Mary's month. The house community in Limburg used to make a procession every day to the Lourdes grotto, where they sang some hymns to our Lady. On one occasion Fr Kolb was standing next to Fr Kentenich. ''I can still remember how as a young novice Fr Kentenich joined in singing to our Lady with his beautiful melodious voice.''

Before he reached his goal of the priesthood, he had to overcome another serious obstacle. Before ordination, each candidate has to be expressly admitted to ordination by his superiors. Young Kentenich was due to make his perpetual profession in September 1909, so that he could then be ordained. The Provincial Council, which had to consider his case, consisted of five priests. When the vote was taken, three were against and two for his admission. Why? No one doubted his intellectual gifts (he was always the best in the class), or his religious nature. They simply did not know, however, what was going on inside him. There was something mysterious about him. The superiors had realised this, but they could not get behind his secret. During the lectures he often asked questions, and on more than one occasion these had cornered his professors. They suspected that he could have genuine problems with believing. If this was so, they could not be sure whether he would remain faithful to his vocation. In addition, there was a final question, his attitude to his superiors. It was feared that once he was ordained he might turn out to be a rebel. All this gave rise to uncertainty in the superiors about his future. As Rector of the house and member of the provincial council, Fr Kolb had to pass on this dramatic news. He was very sorry to have to do so, because he was fond of the novice.

Have you heard the results of the council meeting?
Yes!
What have you to say to it?
God's providence!
What do you intend to do?
First of all get my matriculation.

Fr Kolb looked at him standing before him – calm, pale and sickly. But he did not cry. "Tears came into my eyes," Fr Kolb related later, "and I sent him off, advising him to do nothing for the present. I considered how the decision could be rescinded." It has to be kept in mind that at that time non-admission to profession meant that no other religious community would take him on. No bishop would be prepared to take him into a seminary and give him another chance, still less to ordain him. In short, his way to the priesthood had been closed forever. Lay theologians were unknown. His whole future disintegrated before him.

The calm and composure with which the young cleric received this dramatic news impressed Fr Kolb. It moved him to raise the question of young Kentenich once more with the provincial council. In the meantime he discussed the matter privately with one of the counsellors and got him to change his mind. The next vote resulted in the admission of Brother Kentenich with three for and two against. What a strange paradox of fate! The man who was destined to be one of the best-known priests in Germany in the 20th century was only admitted to ordination with grave reservations. However, all the obstacles had been overcome and young Kentenich approached his goal.

Two months before his ordination, on the feast of the Queen of the Apostles 1910, he gave a talk to the house community at Limburg on Mary's rôle in the history of the Church. "How fortunate," he said, "is he who may give his whole strength directly for the holy cause in the battle raging around Mary's standard; how fortunate is he who with apostolic sincerity may offer the merits of the work of his hands, his studies, his sacrifices, his suffering, to Mary, so that our Patroness may protect us as we fight in the front lines and bless her work with plentiful success."

On 8 July that year Bishop Heinrich Vieter, Vicar Apostolic of the Cameroons, solemnly laid his hands on

Joseph Kentenich, making him a priest forever. Among the few photos that exist of this time there is one that was taken on Fr Kentenich's ordination day itself. Whoever looks at it sees the traces of long years of severe inner battles in the clear and penetrating gaze of the twenty-five-year-old, in the firm line of his lips and in the restrained strength of his whole bearing, but one can also discover his inner conviction that he had a great mission. Two days later he celebrated his first Holy Mass in the chapel of the Mission House at Limburg. The sentences he had printed on his ordination card reveal the great features of his future work, "Grant, O my God, that all minds may be united in the truth and all hearts in love". The two ejaculations that follow, "Heart of Jesus, I trust in you", and "Sweet heart of Mary, be my salvation", when seen in the light of his future work as a priest, reveal an essential component of his charism and his Marian mission. He knew that he had been called to proclaim the indissoluble unity, the two-in-oneness of Christ and Mary, in the whole work of redemption.

4. THE FOUNDATION

After his ordination, Fr Kentenich still had to complete
a year of studies, because it was the practice at that time
to ordain candidates to the priesthood at the end of their
third theology year. When he had completed his studies
in September 1911, he was appointed German and Latin
Master at the Pallottine Minor Seminary. So he moved
to Ehrenbreitstein opposite Coblenz on the right bank
of the Rhine. The syllabus for his subjects was laid down.
However, the young teacher embarked on new methods.
(Fr Kolb, who had made the appointment, wrote in his
memoirs: "He gladly took on this task, but he immediately set about it in his own way.") The typical
teaching method of that time was that the teacher kept
a marked distance from the boys, a great deal had to be
learnt by heart, and the lessons showed little dynamic
life. Fr Kentenich regarded himself not only as a teacher,
but also as an educator. "You are not only a teacher, but
also an educator," he wrote in one of his personal jottings. Such an idea was innate to him. It was for this
reason that he looked upon his appointment as an opportunity to carry out what he regarded as his mission.
"As far back as I can remember, I have always seen it
clearly and taken it for granted that I must create the new
man, who is not dependent on empty phrases, who can
decide for himself, and who can go his own way free from
outward drill."
When he began teaching, the boys noticed that they did
not have just another teacher before them, but a person
motivated by a deep conviction, who was imbued with

a great ideal. "So we want to get down to work together," he said. "I shall demand a lot of you, but you may also make the highest demands on me. And so we shall become good friends in the coming year." This was a quite extraordinary statement for a teacher to make in that time of exaggerated and rigid formalism. He did not offer the boys just any form of friendship. As a priest he wanted to be a fatherly friend. He saw clearly that he was a person in authority and had to exercise his authority, but his aim was not to suppress life, he rather wanted to awaken it, let it grow and then channel it correctly. Among his personal jottings we find the following: "As a teacher be a fatherly friend to your boys.

a) While teaching:

basic character: dignified seriousness, moderate, but inexorable in making demands (. . .).

You have most authority if your knowledge is precise, if it is presented clearly, if you are consistent in your demands and in the way you treat the boys."

He tried to enter into a dialogue with the boys and to get them to participate actively in the lessons. He educated them to be independent in their thinking and actions. This meant, for example, that they should not simply learn grammar rules by heart, and then repeat them, they should rather work out for themselves the fundamental principles of such rules. Education towards independence presupposes that a sense of personal responsibility has been awakened, and that the teacher trusts the pupils. This was the reason why he used to leave the classroom when the boys were writing class tests. He gave the theme and then left the boys alone to work it out. Although he spent only a year at Ehrenbreitstein, his personality and his activity had a very profound effect. One of the boys of that time, later Father Kastner, recalled decades later, ''His lessons were not drilled into us in the usual way, instead they thoroughly mobilised all the mental and moral forces of the individual and the class community as a whole in a free, noble and well-disciplined competition of minds''.

When he was not teaching he had little contact with the boys. Other priests had this task. Whatever spare time he had was spent in helping out in the surrounding parishes. He felt a special preference for the most needy lay people, for those who kept their distance from the Church. ''I wanted to have nothing to do with you in order to be able to devote all my remaining time and strength to the service of people in the world, in particular the old and hardened sinners. I wanted to hunt down the so-called 'Easter lambs', and my greatest joy as a priest was when one came along so heavily laden with the age-old lumber that had collected over the years that the kneeler in the confessional creaked.'' It seems that this is a feature of the twenty-six-year-old priest that was to mark his entire priestly life – he wanted to be a transparency of the merciful love of God, the Father. This man who could make radical demands, who always reached out only to the highest ideals, could at the same time be merciful towards human weakness.

In the following year he was appointed Spiritual Director of the College at Schoenstatt. In September 1912 the senior classes had been moved from Ehrenbreitstein to Schoenstatt, part of the small town of Vallendar on the Rhine. This change was the cause of great dissatisfaction among the boys. They had enjoyed a fair amount of freedom in Ehrenbreitstein, but in the new house strict discipline was introduced. The relationship of trust between the boys and the masters broke down. As a result, the administration of the house began to look around for a suitable priest for the post of Spiritual Director. The Provincial, Fr Kolb, immediately thought of Fr Kentenich, but he did not want to transfer him from his teaching post at Ehrenbreitstein. However, when two other priests appointed to the post fell ill in rapid succession, he finally decided to entrust Fr Kentenich with the office. Fr Kentenich himself had had nothing to do with the decision, so he interpreted it as being the expression of God's will. "I have, therefore, submitted," he told the boys, "and I am firmly resolved to carry out all my duties to you all and to each one individually as perfectly as possible."

As a man who allowed himself to be directed by clear principles, he always sought to discover God's plan in everything. He regarded the ordinary events and circumstances of life as an expression of God's will. Since he was highly sensitive to the supernatural, he was able to discern what God wanted. Once there was clarity on a matter for him, he committed himself wholly to it. "I now place myself completely at your disposal with all that I am and have – my knowledge and ignorance, my abilities and disabilities, but above all my heart," he told the boys after his appointment.

This opening talk of 27 October 1912 has gone down in Schoenstatt's history as the "Pre-founding Document". In it Fr Kentenich gave a clear and precise description of the reason for their gathering, "Under Mary's protection we want to learn how to educate ourselves to become firm, free and priestly characters''. Here we have in germ the great aim of the Schoenstatt Movement, the education of the ''new man in the new community''. From the first Fr Kentenich tried to educate personalities that are capable of exercising genuine freedom. That is to say, personalities that can withstand the pressures of the world around them, who are able and in a position to come to a personal decision and then to translate that decision into action. This is the exact counterpart to the mass-man, whom Fr Kentenich described as the person ''who does what others do, because others do it''. The World War that broke out two years later, drawing many of these young men onto the battlefields, was to confirm the rightness of this intuition. The battle for freedom has become a golden thread that can be followed up throughout Schoenstatt's history and all the founder's struggles.

What is meant is true freedom, the freedom of God's children, which does not consist in doing the things one feels like doing just now, or that suddenly come to mind, but in doing what one should, what God wants one to do. It is being ''free from'' and ''free for'': free from all that is contrary to the divine, in order to be free for all that is divine, and in this way to carry out God's will. The way to this high goal is concrete and difficult. It must be practicable in everyday life. It is the way of self-education.

How did Fr Kentenich come to this conclusion? He was an attentive and vigilant observer of life. (''I have learnt more from personally observing life, than from studying books,'' he once said of himself.) That is why he explained to the boys that we do not need to have very

39

much knowledge of the world and of people in order to realise clearly that despite all its progress and its discoveries our time is unable to save people from the experience of inner emptiness. The reason for this is that all our attention and activity is exclusively devoted to the macrocosm, the great world around us. "There is, however, a world that is eternally old and yet remains eternally new – the microcosm, the world in miniature, our own inner world, which remains unknown and unexplored."

His diagnosis penetrated still more deeply. It uncovered the root of the evil. "Our dominion over the gifts and forces of nature outside ourselves has not gone hand in hand with the subjugation of the elemental and bestial forces in our human breast. This tremendous dichotomy, this immeasurable gulf, is constantly becoming bigger and more abysmal...." Not content with making a purely situational analysis, he immediately set up a programme of action. "The measure of our progress in the sciences must be the measure of our growth in inner depth, our spiritual growth." If we do not do this, a tremendous emptiness will make its presence felt within us, an abyss that will make us very unhappy. Hence self-education. And this task is very consciously placed "under Mary's protection".

This twenty-seven-year-old priest had made up his mind to tackle a task that would influence the future and reach very far afield. For it he needed an organization in keeping with the circumstances, "a sort of Marian Sodality such as exists at various Colleges and Universities".

The whole undertaking should become their common work. The idea had originated with Fr Kentenich, but he did not want to carry it out without the co-operation of his boys. This dimension of togetherness became a central feature of his whole work. The "new community" grows out of common responsibility. As early as 1912 he said, "We want to create this organization. We – not I! Because I shall do nothing in this regard, absolutely nothing, without your complete agreement. (...) I am convinced that we shall bring about something useful if we all co-operate."

The idea of founding a Marian Sodality for the boys was at first not welcomed by the superiors. They feared the formation of a parallel organization to that of the house. Fr Kentenich had to put off the execution of his plan for some time, but he did not give it up. To start with he encouraged the formation of a "Mission Association". The superiors had no objections to that, because the Pallottines had opened the seminary in order to educate missionaries for the Cameroons. Fr Kentenich gave regular talks to the boys, as well as what were called "the Instructions". Meanwhile developments continued, and by the beginning of 1914 the superiors were prepared to agree to the foundation of a Marian Sodality. However, this goal was not to be attained without many battles. The boys who wanted to join the Sodality met with prejudiced objections on the part of the other boys, and these had first to be convinced of the advantages of transforming the Mission Association into a Marian Sodality. The 25 March, the feast of the Annunciation, was the appointed day for the foundation. In the meantime, however, Fr Kentenich was admitted to hospital at the end of February with a serious lung disease. (By the way, it is quite remarkable to notice that at decisive moments in Schoenstatt's history, Fr Kentenich underwent a physical breakdown.) The foundation had to be postponed to 19 April, Low Sunday.

In the address he gave on that day, he told the young and enthusiastic sodalists, "We have come here of our own accord. *We* were the insistent petitioners. We may never forget this. Only when our superiors were convinced of the honesty of our striving and of our moral maturity, would they give the permission we had asked for." He then pointed to the main goal of the Sodality, to find Jesus and Mary. In the process he underlined the fact that the ultimate goal is not Mary, but Jesus. "We are consecrating ourselves without reserve to the ever blessed Virgin, so that she may lead us to her divine Son. (...) Through Mary to Jesus. That is the whole purpose of the Sodality put as briefly as possible."

A great step forward had been taken. The reader may perhaps be under the impression that the foundation of a Marian Sodality is something for sentimental and weak souls, something for young girls; attachment to Mary could all too easily lead to a certain passivity. Fr Kentenich saw things differently. He expected exactly the opposite result from his boys' deep attachment to Mary. In his opinion there is hardly a more important or more effective means of education than genuine love for Mary. Why? Because "she mobilises whatever chivalry and manliness we possess and brings them to their full unfolding. Only when with the best will in the world and the use of all our abilities we really cannot manage, will she help us to overcome our difficulties."

While the boys in Schoenstatt were aglow with their

Marian ideals, Europe was living in ever-growing tension. Once the Balkan crisis had been overcome, the future warring powers began an arms race. On 28 June the Archduke Franz-Ferdinand and the Princess of Hohenberg were assassinated at Sarajevo, the capital city of Bosnia. The boys in Schoenstatt were already thinking about their summer holidays. In the valley, surrounded by tall trees, two Romanesque towers, the last remains of an Augustinian convent of the twelfth century, overlooked the surrounding landscape. Not far away was an old two-storey house. Facing it was a neglected little chapel where the garden tools were stored at that time. In their search for a suitable room for their meetings, the sodalists hit upon the idea of using this neglected little chapel. They presented their case to the Rector of the house, and in July received the permission they requested. And so they set to, in order to make it presentable again.

On 18th of the same month, a copy of the "Allgemeine Rundschau" came into Fr Kentenich's possession. An article by Fr Cyprian Fröhlich related the history of the Italian Marian Shrine at Valle di Pompeii. This place of pilgrimage had not come into existence as a result of an apparition of Our Lady, as had Lourdes or Fatima. It owed its origin to the sacrifices and activity of the Italian lawyer, Bartolo Longo. This report was a sign from Divine Providence, a hint that required interpretation. Was it not possible that something similar could happen to the ancient chapel of St Michael? Was not the Mother of God looking for a human instrument — as she had at Pompeii — who would be willing to co-operate with her in carrying out her plans?

On 27 July Austria declared war on Serbia. On 1 August Germany declared war on Russia, and, two days later, on France. Finally England broke off relations with Germany. The great European war had broken out. It was to spread and become the First World War. As far as Fr Kentenich was concerned, nothing happened by chance. God was speaking in all that happened. Our part consists in hearing his voice, interpreting it and answering it. According to the Second Vatican Council it is the task of the People of God to undertake this prophetic activity, in that "it labours to decipher authentic signs of God's presence and purpose in the happenings, needs and desires in which this People has a part along with other men of our age. For faith throws a new light on everything (and) manifests God's designs . . .". (The Church Today, II.)

The boys returned from their holidays in October. On the 18th of that month Fr Kentenich gave them a talk that has since come to be known as the "Founding Document". In it he tried to interpret the signs of the times. He realised that a new epoch was approaching "with giant strides". The speeding up of history by the war became a programme: "Speeding up the development of our self-sanctification and as a result transforming our little chapel into a pilgrimage chapel." He tried to make full use of the impulses generated by the war by placing them in the service of the Christian life. "I am . . . firmly convinced that each one of us could join in the battle and victory, could help to give advice in the highest Council of War, and could help to build world history. We are not just useless numbers condemned to idle inactivity, but essential factors with a very important part to play. The weapon, the sword, with which we are to help our Fatherland to victory, is serious, strict penance, self-discipline, overcoming self: self-sanctification.''

He told them in the form of a modest ''wish'' about one of his ''favourite ideas'' upon which he had reflected again and again in the past months. Taking the scene on Mount Tabor as his starting point (when Jesus was transfigured before Peter, James and John), he made a comparison and asked, ''Would it not be possible for our Sodality chapel to become at the same time our Tabor where Mary's glories are revealed?'' And he continued, ''without doubt we could not achieve a greater apostolic deed, nor leave a more precious legacy to our successors, than if we were to prevail upon our Queen and Mistress to set up her throne here in a special way, to distribute her treasures and work miracles of grace. You can guess what I am aiming at – I want to make this place into a place of pilgrimage, a place of grace.'' The talk came to an end. The boys scattered. Outwardly nothing of any note had taken place. It was as though the seed had fallen into the ground and disappeared. And yet this 18 October was to leave its mark on history. Heaven had again touched the earth, God had touched man. Mary, the Mother of God, had taken a new initiative in salvation history. And the human partner answered in a simple, childlike way with a leap of faith. Fr Kentenich was later to acknowledge that this was the most difficult step of his life, because his faith could only discover a fine ray of light in the darkness. As time went by he would have to take more painful decisions, but by then he was able to base himself on repeated experiences of God's working.

5. CHILDREN OF WAR

When he was speaking to the Schoenstatt Family, Fr Kentenich often repeated the expression, "We are children of war". He based his statement on the fact that Schoenstatt came into existence in 1914, and its foundation coincided with the outbreak of World War 1. However, this statement also gives expression to a fundamental principle: There can be no redemption without a battle, without opposition, without blood being shed. In a letter he wrote in 1939, Fr Kentenich spoke of a "building principle" of the family, according to which we "as children of war can only grow and flourish in battle and war, in trial and persecution". But let us return to 1914.

The results of the war could be felt everywhere, as well as at Schoenstatt. One of the boys recalls, "In 1915 we returned from Ehrenbreitstein to Schoenstatt. The college had been turned into a military hospital. Down in the valley we lived in extreme poverty. We had neither beds nor furniture. The sum total of our possessions consisted in some straw sacks piled one on top of the other and a box in which we stored our things. The mice ran around beside us. . . ."

Even in the first days of the war some of the Schoenstatt Sodalists were called up for active service. Fr Kentenich had to face new challenges. How were they to remain in contact with the men at the front and uphold Schoenstatt's ideals? Besides fostering their attachment to the place Schoenstatt – to the shrine, to the Sodality and to the Spiritual Director – he undertook two strategic measures: an intensive correspondence with one another, and the foundation of a periodical, which appeared under the title "Mater ter Admirabilis". He spared himself no effort. His sole desire was to remain in contact with them. "Perhaps you are already lying in the trenches," he wrote in June 1915. "Be that as it may, cherish the firm trust that our dear heavenly Mother will still lead all our sodalists who really have a vocation to their goal, despite the apparent impossibility." From this he went on to explain the name of the picture they had hung up in the little chapel. "We have called it the Mater ter Admirabilis, Mother Thrice Admirable. This is the title by which we shall honour her in our Sodality chapel in future. For she has without doubt shown that she is wonderful to our soldier-sodalists, and not least to you."

The periodical which first appeared on 5 March 1916 was the result of Fr Kentenich's initiative. Its aim was to offer spiritual support and inspiration to the sodalists who were exposed to the dangers and breaking tests of army life in the war. As has so often happened, it began with a modest issue of a hundred copies. Even by the end of the year its circulation had risen to a thousand. And by December 1917 the subscription number had risen to two thousand. The publisher had taken a risk, now he was reaping the fruits. "Many of you, dear Sodalists," he wrote on the first anniversary of the foundation of the periodical, "can still remember how hesitantly and timidly we prepared the first hundred copies a year ago. It cost daring, because fifty would have been sufficient for our soldier-sodalists at that time."

It was the means by which the life of the Marian Sodality at Schoenstatt was spread far beyond its own walls. Thus, for example, the Prefect of a Marian Sodality in Holland wrote to Fr Kentenich and asked him to send a copy of the MTA to all his sodalists at the front. Fr Kentenich and his work became increasingly well-known through the periodical. At the beginning of 1917, Professor Rademacher of Bonn University mentioned Schoenstatt at a Congress for the Pastoral Care of Youth as an "outstanding example". He based this statement on material from the periodical "MTA".

From those far off days of World War 1 until the day of his death, that is, in a period covering more than fifty years, Fr Kentenich built up a gigantic work step by step. He devoted himself completely to it, day and night. He took note of every event that happened, great and small, he was attentive to every person who came across his way. He took great pains to discover the structure of things and an explanation of the order of being. In everything he picked up a message from God or recognised God's wish being revealed to him. This was typical of the way he worked – his plans were not in the first place his own brain-wave, but designs or attempts to grasp and express God's great plan in which he believed unwaveringly. If things were not completely clear, he usually waited until a sign had made God's will obvious to him. That is why throughout his long life he practised the virtue of obedience to an extraordinary degree. (During his homily at Fr Kentenich's funeral on 20 September 1968, Bishop Heinrich Tenhumberg of Münster said, "I have never known any other person of whom I was so convinced that at every moment he was listening, listening to God, and was therefore at bottom an obedient person".)

In 1915 a new expression found its way into the Marian Sodality, "contributions to the capital of grace". What did it mean? How had it originated? On 18 October 1914, when Fr Kentenich presented his "favourite idea" to the boys of transforming the chapel in the valley into a place of pilgrimage, he made its fulfilment dependent on one condition: the serious striving of every sodalist to become holy. The efforts and sacrifices this required were to be placed at our Lady's disposal in the shrine. ("In this way the Sodality chapel should become the cradle of sanctity for us. This holiness will exert gentle force on our heavenly Mother and draw her down to us.") The expression may at first sound materialistic, because whoever hears the word "capital" today, spontaneously associates it with money. But the expression also has a theological foundation. It is based on the reality of the Mystical Body of Christ, to which all the baptised belong, and on the communion of saints, that is, on the exchange of goods and merits within the Church. It is based on the words of our Lord, "Store up treasures for yourselves in heaven, where neither moth nor woodworms destroy them and thieves cannot break in and steal" (Matthew 6: 20; Luke 12: 33); it is based on the teaching of the Apostle Paul, "You were called together as parts of one body" (Col. 3: 15); "So death is at work in us, but life in you" (2 Cor. 4: 12); "It makes me happy to suffer for you, as I am suffering now, and in my own body to do what I can to make up all that has still to be undergone by Christ for the sake of his body, the Church" (Col. 1: 24).

In the years that followed Fr Kentenich changed the original text of the talk of 18.10.1914 slightly and added formulations that reflected the life of the Sodality. "Through the faithful and most faithful fulfilment of their duties" they should earn "a great many merits" and place them at our Lady's disposal. In 1919 the text read: "Diligently bring me contributions to the capital of grace." This formulation was to be the object of fierce attacks in the 1930's and gave rise to a controversy that caused the Schoenstatt Family to reflect more deeply on the foundation and importance of these "contributions". In a letter he wrote for the twenty-fifth anniversary of Schoenstatt's foundation, Fr Kentenich explained, "In essentials our Family came into existence through the contributions to the capital of grace of the Mater ter Admirabilis. Therefore it must uphold them without wavering at all times, but very particularly when it is being tested by fire. With them (the contributions) stands and falls the Family and its fruitfulness."

A person who had understood all this most profoundly and lived it, was a sodalist belonging to the founder generation: Josef Engling. He was born on 5 January 1898 at Prositten (Ermland, now part of Poland), the son of a farmer. Even as a very small child he was remarkable for his piety. When he was twelve, he began to write a diary in preparation for his First Holy Communion. His family read the "Stern von Afrika" (The Star of Africa), a periodical published by the Pallottine Fathers at Limburg.

He came to Schoenstatt in the winter of 1912/13. Father and son had spent two days on the train. It was obvious that he was not brilliant; he was not the most talented or the most athletic. And yet he soon stood out among his classmates; he distinguished himself for his noble-mindedness and his idealism, for his piety and his persevering efforts to educate himself. In whatever concerned the Sodality he was soon Fr Kentenich's right hand. In November 1916, he and ten others were called up to the army. On the 19th of that month he wrote in his war diary (this was a custom with many sodalists who were called up) "... Child, do not forget your Mother! Those were the last words of Fr Kentenich's talk. Then with firm voices we renewed our consecration to Mary, and an hour later we had left Schoenstatt, which we had come to love so much. We were accompanied for a long time by the gaze of the other sodalists." His first posting was to the military barracks at Hagenau near Strassburg in Elsass, where he received his military training. He wrote to Fr Kentenich every fortnight from there and reported on his spiritual life and apostolic activity. Fr Kentenich answered him, supported him and sent him reading matter. Josef thanked him in reply, "A sincere thank you for the wonderful thoughts about love for our dear little Mother.* It touched the hearts. Only one thought shall rule my whole life: all for you, dear little Mother!" To start with, the war brought him to the Russian front. His company was stationed at Jablonna, in the Warsaw area. From August to November 1917 he was at the front. At the end of December his company left Tarnopol and on 5 January 1918 reached Dun in France. Even in the midst of the hardships of a soldier's life –

* The use of the diminutive form is an expression of especial intimacy and endearment more current in Eastern Europe than in the West.

mud, cold, hunger, tiredness, dangers, the battle of nerves at the front – Josef lived the ideals of his Marian Sodality. On more than one occasion he had to bear the taunts and teasing of his comrades because of his religious convictions, which he did not try to hide. In the end, however, he won their respect and admiration as a soldier. "In him I met a true character, a man of action with an unbroken will and yet great amiability." His rucksack contained not only his full military pack, but also some books and writing materials.

He conducted an intense correspondence with the other sodalists. At times he wrote with fingers swollen from the cold or by the light of a glimmering lamp. "We may not give in. I am utterly determined: aut Caesar aut nihil! Only those who really want it are capable of working for a spiritual renewal. The world needs men who are real men with rock-like wills and boundless love."

In the confusion of the war he lived an intense spiritual life, which found practical expression in a spiritual daily order controlled in writing. His relationship to his Spiritual Director was a decisive factor in his inner growth. Once, when he was on the Western Front and was having a spiritual retreat, he came to the decision, "I shall become holy through my Spiritual Director!" At the close of each day he in spirit asked him for his blessing. His letters to Fr Kentenich show his spiritual progress. Thus, on 20 May 1918, he wrote, "Today I am having a day of spiritual renewal. In the course of the day I recalled my former zeal for the Sodality and the time at Schoenstatt, and I promised my little Mother that I would become just as zealous again. The same should happen to my love for my neighbour. A few days ago, as the shells fell to left and right of me, I prayed as usual to my little Mother and visited the shrine in spirit. I felt so close to my beloved little Mother to an extent I have never experienced before in my life. Her nearness was so sweet to me, so delightful, and I did not feel the least anxiety about the shells. It was such a happy state, one in which I would have liked to remain forever. How beautiful and sublime, how lovable our dear Mater ter Admirabilis is, and how much confidence she inspires! I am often overcome by great longing for her shrine, for you and my dear fellow-students''.

In July 1918 he spent a few weeks on leave. He first paid a visit to his parents at home in Prositten. On his return journey to France he halted for a few days at Schoenstatt. There he was able to talk to Fr Kentenich in peace for quite some time. He used the time to have a private retreat. On 30 July he took final leave of Schoenstatt. Before he left he knelt down and asked Fr Kentenich for his blessing. Then he went to the shrine, and from there made his way to Vallendar. Fr Kentenich accompanied him. He said good bye to Josef for the last time with the customary greeting, ''Nos cum prole pia'', to which he received the answer, ''Benedicat Virgo Maria'' (Mother, with your loving Son, bless us each and every one). He had just left when his friend, Karl Burg, arrived in Schoenstatt. ''It is a pity you didn't come a little earlier,'' Fr Kentenich told him, ''you would have met Josef. I am sure you would have been edified by him. He has matured. His look is so clear.''

In the months that followed, as the German front gradually crumbled, Josef Engling's character reached full maturity. In August and September 1918 he was allowed to experience God's presence very profoundly. Fr Kentenich followed these developments through the letters he received, and recognised the special guidance of the Holy Spirit. "I would strongly support the inspiration of grace that is urging you to be very strict with yourself; you have realised very clearly that you could have progressed further thanks to all the graces God and our dear Mother have given you. I consider it one of their greatest kindnesses that you are again striving for your old aim, to become a saint, with all your old enthusiasm and zest, despite the great difficulties military life faces you with." Josef fell in battle on 4 October that year, struck in the head by shrapnel not far from Cambrai. A few months prior to this he had made the offer of his life to our Lady and she had accepted his offer. ("if, however, it can be reconciled with your plans, let met be a sacrifice for the tasks you have set our sodality," he wrote in a prayer on 3 June 1918.) We are told that when Fr Kentenich received the news of Josef's death, he closed his eyes for a moment, then he said. "Now the Sodality has its first saint". Josef Engling was dead, but that was not the end of everything. For Fr Kentenich, whose practical faith in Divine Providence endeavoured to discover God's plans behind everything, Josef Engling's heroic life was inexplicable from a purely human point of view. God's influence was very clear. In the oblation of this life he saw the first important sign that the courageous step he had taken on 18 October 1914 had been accepted by heaven. That is why he later made the statement that in his life Josef Engling had "lived the Founding Document and anticipated the founding history".

Once the war had ended the sodalists returned to Schoenstatt. But they were no longer alone. While living at such close quarters with their comrades-at-arms at the front they had passed on their ideals. A number had joined the Schoenstatt Sodality without deciding to become candidates to the priesthood. They met on 20 August 1919 at Dortmund-Hörde and founded the ''Apostolic Union''. Fr Kentenich had naturally been invited to the gathering. At first he accepted the invitation, but at the last moment he declined. This surprised them greatly. One of the participants later commented on the incident, ''The Spiritual Director was not personally present at Hörde. He considered it more advisable – and today we can see that he was right not to come – for us to show how much the undertaking meant to us. Some sodalists had come from Schoenstatt and had brought some guidelines from Fr Kentenich with them.''

It was then that Fr Kentenich was released from all other duties so that he could devote himself wholly to the work in Schoenstatt. He moved to the nearby village of Engers, where he served a community of sisters as chaplain. This was a decisive turning-point. ''With that I had set off on a course that would lead past every kind of abyss, through darkness and night, along totally unknown ways, to the highest heights.'' If these words are taken literally, they give some idea of the daring that characterised Fr Kentenich's life. It was as though he had to pay the price of constant daring in order to build up his work. ''The only thread by which I could orientate myself was the thread of faith in Divine Providence, which led me onwards, ever further, one little step after the other. Whoever knows the conditions in the world, the Church, and in society at that time can guess how hazardous the whole undertaking was. . . . It meant creating a great, a tremendously great and new world out of nothing, as it were . . .'' Shortly after moving from Vallendar to Engers, Fr Kentenich became so ill that it was feared that he would die. ''The adventure grew in magnitude, risk and enormity because I was seriously ill at the time. When I moved into the hospital at Engers, I was received and treated as someone about to die. They expected my physical collapse at any moment. This didn't disturb me in the least. My body practically did not exist for me. I worked day and night and lived in great and world-wide plans. I had to feel my way carefully in little things, as in the great, to discover the ways Divine Providence was opening up before me for the realization of these gigantic plans. Because everything I had in mind as an ideal seemed so daring and utterly strange in the world, I was forced to bear it as a secret in my heart. It was only here and there on occasion that I revealed what was in me and lifted the veil slightly from my world. With whatever I undertook I was not interested in success. I was quite satisfied with the certainty in mind and heart that I was working to carry out a divine plan.''

6. SILENT GROWTH

From nature we can learn that all that is alive grows slowly, silently, without haste, yet constantly. Since Fr Kentenich believed that he had not been called to create an organization, in the first place, but rather a movement of life, he referred time and again to this "law of organic growth". In this context he liked to refer to a saying of Nietzsche, who pointed out that the quiet hours are often the most important and fruitful ones. Accordingly his work grew gradually. With the agreement of his superiors he moved to Engers in October 1920. He lived in the Augustinian convent there and cared for the Franciscan Sisters of Waldbreitbach. This task left him with much spare time which he could use for the inspiration and leadership of the growing Schoenstatt Movement. That year it grew in two directions: The Apostolic League was founded and women were admitted for the first time.

The young men had founded the Apostolic Union the previous year. This was an élite community setting high demands, and its task consisted in working like leaven in all the Catholic organizations for men. The Apostolic League, for its part, had fewer fixed demands to fulfil, and this made it possible for the Schoenstatt Movement to have a far wider circle of influence. This was decisive for its structural universality. In order to secure this wideranging influence, it was not only necessary to have an élite, the possibility had also to exist for people to join the movement more spontaneously and less formally. In order to offer these members spiritual guidance, Fr

Kentenich started the periodical "Königin der Apostel" (Queen of the Apostles) in March 1921.

The second growth-ring was the admission of women to the Schoenstatt Movement. Until that time Fr Kentenich had not involved himself in the pastorate for women. He had consciously refrained from taking on the pastoral care of women until he had turned thirty-five. The reason for such a resolution is obvious: in order to approach women with a thoroughly fatherly attitude, sufficient human maturity is required. And in fact, Providence did intend that from this year until his death (he died immediately after celebrating Holy Mass, which was attended by about six hundred Sisters of Mary), he should be a true father to hundreds, indeed thousands of women, and that through their meeting with him they should come to experience the reality of the world of childlikeness, of being a child. "Then in 1920/21 the women came into the Movement. A Miss B, a teacher in the Palatinate, had heard something about Schoenstatt, and wrote to ask whether women would be accepted. Now at the time we were a young community, there was absolutely no place for expansion.... The talks I gave in Engers to the sisters were my preparatory school for the pastorate for women. I told Miss B that she might join the League. The women sat in on the talks for the theology students." On 8 December 1920 Countess von Boullion and her cousin, Maria Christmann, were the first to consecrate themselves to the MTA in the shrine. In August the following year there was a congress for women, and thirty-five took part.

It is impressive to see all that Fr Kentenich did for women and their world in the course of the years. A study written during the first years of his priesthood concerns itself with the problems confronting modern woman. With intuitive certainty he worked out the core of the matter as follows: "Our era has the task to determine and to define the position of woman for the future in keeping with the changed circumstances of our age." He insisted on the necessity of educating woman to be a personality. He argued the case for the admission of women to higher studies (we take it for granted today, but at that time it was anything but usual). His concern was to determine the "rôle" of woman for the future. In keeping with his method of tackling such subjects, he insisted that two essential and complementary features had to be considered: What is the permanent, the essential, the "metaphysical" element in woman? And what can and must change in adaptation to the new circumstances of the age? It was completely foreign to him to favour change for the sake of change, or to propagate what is known as Women's Lib today. What he wanted was really free women in the deepest sense of the word. After all, the battle for true freedom, the "freedom of God's children", is one of Schoenstatt's goals. And women could only become free to the extent they discovered their own original character and mission. For almost fifty years (from 1920 – 1968) Fr Kentenich regarded it as his mission to get to know the feminine soul, to study the eternal, the metaphysical in woman, and to allow a new type of woman to take on living form. He was helped in carrying out this great and noble task by the fact that he combined in himself to an uncommon degree the qualities of a born psychologist, a genuine metaphysician, and, above all, a man of God.

He was a true pioneer in the field of woman's education. He worked untiringly to help women to discover their real identity, to value themselves in a sound manner, and to take up their rôle in God's plan and in salvation history. Through meditating on our Lady he discovered the "Eternal in woman", the ideal of womanhood. And so he always tried to lead women to see Mary as their ideal ("the sun-clad image of feminine nobility, greatness and dignity"). He considered it his task "to see to it that the image of God's Mother is always clearly seen as the sun-clad image, the perfect, the soul-imbued ideal of woman". Since he was a realist with great foresight, he was well aware that the fulfilment of such a task would sooner or later be connected with calumnies and slander. And that is what happened. "It is natural that all sorts of difficulties are awaiting us in the course of time. 'When I am raised up on the cross, I shall draw all things to myself.' Whoever wants to redeem the world with our Saviour, must stand under his cross." He wrote these words to Sr Emilie Engel. On occasion he could say that despite everything he would consider himself fortunate if he had managed to imprint Mary's features on at least *one* woman.

The Church of our days still has a tremendous task to achieve in this sphere. It is an accepted part of the life of Christian people to honour and invoke Mary as Mother, Intercessor and Queen. But there is still another dimension that has to be discovered: the image of Mary that is not time-bound, but which is at the same time timely, forever timely. Pope Paul VI was referring to this problem in his Apostolic Exhortation "Marialis cultus" (1974), when he noted that it was possible to discover a certain aversion to devotion to Mary; that many are "finding it difficult to take as an example Mary of Nazareth" (No. 34); and it "cannot easily be reconciled with today's life style, especially with the way women are living today". He states that our era is called upon "to verify its knowledge of reality with the word of God, and ... to compare its anthropological ideas and the problems springing therefrom with the figure of the Virgin Mary as presented by the Gospel" (No. 37).

This had been one of Fr Kentenich's favourite ideas since the 1920's. He never tired of pointing out that love, affection and attachment to the Mother of God on its own is not enough. At the same time, it is necessary for us to become like her and to go through the world at the side of Christ as a "living image of Mary". He formulated his desire with classic brevity in a prayer he made in the concentration camp at Dachau:

"Let us go like you through life,
let us be your living image,
strong and noble, simple, mild,
spreading love, and joy, and concord."

Let us return to the early 1920's. If the foundation of an all-comprising movement was the goal aimed at, women could not be left out. The Movement needed a group, a community of women, who were prepared to dedicate their lives to Schoenstatt, in order to exemplify the ideal image of the new woman and to inspire the formations for women. Fr Kentenich presented this idea during a congress for members of the Women's Apostolic Union in August 1924. The seed fell on good ground. Three girls decided to place themselves wholly at the disposal of the Schoenstatt Movement. In January 1925 they consecrated themselves to the MTA in the shrine. "You are probably not aware of the full importance of the last few days, nor have you probably realised what a significant turning-point has been reached in the history of the Apostolic Union through the foundation of the first sisterhood of the Union to work on a full-time basis at the centre." With the appointment of a superior for the sisterhood in October 1926, the Institute of the Schoenstatt Sisters of Mary had come into existence. Twenty-two years later, in 1948, Rome acknowledged it as one of the first Secular Institutes in the Church.

Since those small beginnings in 1920, Schoenstatt has spread widely among women. We would be quite justified in saying that the feminine sex has received a home in Schoenstatt. Near the original shrine we can find the Sisters of Mary, the Institute of Our Lady of Schoenstatt, the Apostolic Union, the Apostolic League, the Girls and the Mothers, besides the Apostolate for the Sick and the Pilgrims' Circle. Woman has come to Schoenstatt and has found the ideal woman in Mary. From there she goes out into the world and tries to make Mary present in everyday life. At the side of man she is a key figure in the renewal of the world and of culture. As a result of this fundamental insight, Fr Kentenich dared to draw a comparison between the consequences of a lost world war and what a false and misleading image of woman can bring about. Although a world war can cause tremendous suffering to the peoples, in Fr Kentenich's opinion this can hardly be compared to the catastrophic effect of a false image of woman. And, as he saw it, it is more decisive and fruitful for a people to uphold the God-willed ideal of woman in life than to win a whole war.

63

From the start of his pastoral activity, Fr Kentenich had worked with priests and seminarians. In 1911 he was the Latin and German Master in the Minor Seminary of the Pallottines in Ehrenbreitstein; as from 1912 he was Spiritual Director in Schoenstatt; Josef Engling and the other hero sodalists had wanted to become priests.

Step by step he accompanied each individual to his ordination to the priesthood. This quiet and profound activity was later extended to seminaries in various German "Ländern" and dioceses – to Baden, Speyer, Paderborn, Freiburg and Münster; to Württemberg, Bavaria and Silesia. At the same time he conducted training courses and retreats in Schoenstatt. These became famous throughout Germany. In 1929 a total of 542 priests took part in these courses. A year later the number was 1 147, in 1931 there were 1 524 and in 1932 even 2 184. Priests and seminarians, who would later have leading positions in the Church, passed through his hands: Adolf Bolte, Bishop of Fulda; Heinrich Tenhumberg, Bishop of Münster; Cardinal Joseph Wendel of Münich; Cardinal Joseph Höffner of Cologne. What was so attractive about Fr Kentenich? He was a man of God and a man of his times; he knew how to combine the eternal and transcendental with the temporal and the concrete; he lived with his "ear at God's heart and his hand on the pulse of time", as he once characterised himself. There was no event, no trend, no important achievement, that he did not take up and discuss, and to which he did not try to find a fitting answer. A fleeting glance at the themes he tackled during these years will easily confirm this statement:

– The meaning and goal of spiritual direction

thorny road, characterised by the closest attention to every least detail'', he said later on when looking back. ''Please remember, it was not only, or exclusively, the big courses that played a rôle in this. If there had not been the personal and individually toned spiritual direction, all without exception would not have meant much. Exact knowledge about the soul-life of the participants, and constant, vital contact with them, gave the direction for the courses, or, it would be better to say, for the choice of the themes and the individual formulations. It also ensured their effectiveness and fruitfulness.''

Since Fr Kentenich was convinced that God had given him the mission to found a movement for the universal renewal of the Church, he considered it a logical consequence that he had to devote himself to the priests. It would be quite impossible to carry out such an aim without the co-operation of the diocesan clergy. ''All the religious trends that do not at least rest on the shoulders of the secular clergy will, in the long run, be condemned to unfruitfulness.'' This outstandingly priestly feature of his character determined his whole life. We shall later find him sharing the misery of the concentration camp at Dachau with hundreds of priests. We shall find him, already advanced in years, kneeling down to receive the blessing of a newly ordained priest. And finally, we shall find him encouraging priests in their difficulties with fatherly understanding. This widely ranging activity throughout Germany for a period of twenty years or more, during which he was supported by the prayers and sacrifices of the Schoenstatt Family, in particular the Sisters of Mary, fully confirms the truth of the statement made by Archbishop Bornewasser of Trier, ''Fr Joseph

Kentenich has already trained thousands of priests in his retreat courses, and all confirm that these retreats are marked by an extremely strong religious spirit. This means that Fr Kentenich is one of the most important pastors for priests of our days'' (1947). At the beginning of the 1920's Fr Kentenich had his residence in Engers. It was from there that he began his apostolic journeys that were to lead him in the course of the years all over Germany, and after 1947 to many parts of the world. In February 1921 he went to Stuttgart to conduct a course for women. One of those present described him in these words, ''Of medium height, with a full, dark beard, he went to the podium and proclaimed his message to us of the general and special providence of God. In conclusion he gave us a talk on our Lady. His voice had a typical cadence at the end of a sentence…'' He journeyed outside Germany for the first time in 1924, when he went to Gossau, Switzerland. His constantly growing apostolic activity absorbed all his strength.

His health at that time was not exactly robust. He was told that if he did not relax his pace of work somewhat, he could become seriously ill. During a course for leaders in Schoenstatt in January 1920 he was so weak that he was unable to hold the third conference one day. In 1922 he once again had a serious cold. ''What virulent colds you catch!'' wrote Fr Kolb. ''Let's hope this one doesn't go down to your lungs! That would be a pretty mess! I hope you will soon get rid of your cold in Engers. But you really must look after yourself a bit better and not take over and do all sorts of things besides your work. Otherwise you will never recover.'' But the patient did not pay too much attention to his former protector.

Three years later the latter again admonished him to care for his health. "If you break down prematurely, who will continue your work?" We are justified in applying to Fr Kentenich those words of the Apostle Paul to the Corinthians, "I am perfectly willing to spend what I have and to be expended, in the interests of your souls" (2 Cor. 12: 15). He did not slow down his pace of work. And it is an historical fact that precisely through struggling on, constant activity and total commitment to his cause, that his health was increasingly stabilized. What explanation is there for that?

It would be possible to give a number of reasons. What makes us tired and costs so much nervous strength is not so much the work we do, but the fact that we bear so many inner problems and tensions around with us. We could compare ourselves to a car that is driving with its brakes on. Whoever works out of love, and hence joyfully, is less easily tired than the person who is motivated by other reasons. Human ambition was not the mainspring of Fr Kentenich's action; he knew and felt that he was an instrument, and only an instrument, in God's hands. ("God has to do the lion's share in the pastorate. In comparison, what man does is nothing, even if he spends all his strength.") This attitude saved him from unnecessary inner tensions. ("My greatest care is to be endlessly carefree," he used to repeat to certain people who were inclined to worry too much.) Besides this, he possessed great self-control. He limited eating and sleeping to the minimum. This required serious self-discipline. He had, for example, trained himself to stand while giving his talks. This habit, which he had exercised for many years, proved to be a providential preparation for the concentration camp at Dachau, where the prisoners had to stand for hours on the parade ground. When he was a prisoner in Coblenz from September 1941 to March 1942, he had no particular difficulty in bearing all the hardships, and survived four weeks in the "Bunker" (solitary confinement in the dark in what had been a bank safety deposit unit) without damage to body or soul. "How could I have survived the first four weeks," he wrote in a letter of 7 December 1941, "unless like Paul I had constantly been hard on my body" (cf 1 Cor 9: 27). His pace of life and work cannot be explained in purely human terms. Ultimately it is necessary to take into account that divine and superhuman forces were at work in him.

In 1928 the so-called Retreat House was blessed. Archbishop Bornewasser was invited to the ceremonies. In the presence of the large number of guests, Fr Kentenich said in his welcoming address, "It is a lovely dream ... that I like to dream .... Perhaps this dream is of the sort that will someday find fulfilment.... (That this Movement) will spread in the course of the years to the ends of the lands and the seas and beyond, all over the world . . . with the bishop and the Pope at the centre!" This "dream" was gradually to find practical fulfilment. Even as early as 1933, only seven years after the foundation of the Sisters of Mary, the first missionary sisters set off for South Africa. Fr Kentenich had this to say, "When we sent our first sisters overseas, we did so simply out of love for our mission of the world (. . .) No matter whether the confusion at home becomes incredibly great, no matter whether the needs of our compatriots grow continuously, we want to and must always uphold and carefully promote our innate universalism.'' Another focal point of Fr Kentenich's apostolic activity lay in the formation of Catholic educators. We can take this for granted, because if a movement wants to form man as a totality, it must concentrate above all on the field of education. The first educational course was held in Schoenstatt in May 1931. Its theme was: ''General principles for a modern asceticism for youth.'' In his introduction, Fr Kentenich put the ''blame'' for the organization of this course on those who had been coming year after year to Schoenstatt for over a decade, in order to go out afterwards with clear directives and intervene in the intellectual and spiritual controversies of that time. Feeling his way into the situation of the times (the events of the years that followed confirmed his prophetic intuition), he said, ''Great and serious things are at stake. The die will be cast in the next few years. Europe will have a new face. Indeed, the whole world will be formed anew.'' He admitted that because of the heat it was not the best time of the year to undertake such important discussions. However, those present might also not overlook a positive aspect: ''It is the Pentecost season. And if there is any epoch in which God's Spirit, the Holy Spirit, is interested in the forming and moulding of Catholic leaders, it must be in this deeply agitated and confused time.'' Three days later he closed the course with the words, ''If all our activity is not accompanied by loving, sincere prayer, we will be building on sand. A true educator is unthinkable unless he is a man of prayer.''

Schoenstatt, April 1929. During a talk for leaders of the

Students' Movement, Fr Kentenich made an almost incomprehensible statement. It caused amazement, even shock, to many. More than one, who had followed him with interest until then, now turned away from him. "In the shadow of the shrine," he maintained, "the destiny of the Church for the coming years will be decided. A serious statement, an important statement. It almost sounds mad. And yet I shall repeat and intensify it: in the shadow of the shrine the destiny of the Church in Germany and even beyond will be essentially decided for the coming centuries." Didn't such a statement go beyond the limits of reason and sanity? Wasn't it presumptuous? Did Schoenstatt's development give occasion for such a statement? It is true, the first fifteen years had given proof of the seriousness, the depth of life and the apostolic strength of the Movement. Yet this on its own was not enough to answer the above questions satisfactorily. The only real answer has to be sought at an even greater depth, in the sphere of prophetic insight. Were these words the expression of mad human ambition, or was it not rather the case that a man of God had spoken? "No prophecy ever came from man's initiative. When men spoke for God it was the Holy Spirit that moved them" (2 Pet. 1: 21). Fr Kentenich did not take it amiss when someone could not believe his words. But he never withdrew his statement about the "shadow of the shrine".

As from this year, Schoenstatt began to co-operate with the Catholic Association for Young Men in Germany. Fr Kentenich was in close touch with two of its leading figures – Jacob Clemens, the Secretary-General, and Prälat Ludwig Wolker, the President-General. The latter

7. DAVID AND GOLIATH

In his first letter to the Corinthians, Paul explains that God's weakness is stronger than all the power of man (cf 1 Cor. 1: 25). Fr Kentenich and his foundation were to experience that this law of salvation history holds good for all time when they went through overwhelming danger in the years of conflict with the National Socialists. He saw Schoenstatt's history in these years symbolised in the Bible story of the battle between the small David and the giant Goliath (cf 1 Sam 17). "We were the little David," he said later, "and our weapon (stones and sling) was the covenant of love." Time and time again we reminded our Lady, "that it is her task to conquer the devil". For our part we believed ever more firmly in her mission, her power, kindness and faithfulness.

Hitler seized power in 1933. It was a momentous event which set in motion a process that Fr Kentenich followed with great attention. Step by step the National Socialists built up their position of power until they had created a totalitarian system, and had made the country into a great military power. With its demand for the whole-hearted commitment of a person, National Socialism behaved like a pseudo-religion, and so it was inevitable that a clash with the Catholic Church would sooner or later develop. Even the Concordat concluded with the Holy See in July that year could not prevent it. There were not many, even within the hierarchy of the Church, who from the first recognised the fundamental tendencies of the new system. So it happened that

73

Cardinal von Galen, who was later to become famous for his opposition to the dictatorship, once asked himself whether it were not possible to "baptise" National Socialism. Fr Kentenich observed during a conversation that he could find no spot over which they could pour the baptismal waters.

He was not satisfied with merely negative criticism. In keeping with his personal structure, he was able to discover many hints about God's plan by "reading them" from National Socialism. In order to do this he made use of a principle borrowed from Augustine. "We want to make use of the heresies in such a way that the true Catholic teaching is more clearly highlighted against them, and as a result is surer and firmer." Later he himself commented upon and explained the Augustinian principle as follows, "From the negative spirit of the world (Zeitgeist) we have deduced the positive spirit of the times (Geist der Zeit). Out of all the negative currents that constantly surrounded us and penetrated us, we tried to deduce the spirit of the times, that is, what God was wanting to say to us." The National Socialists spoke of heroism and of the necessity to make sacrifices; in reply Fr Kentenich preached for a full year on childlike heroism. He placed the "Schoenstattreich" (realm) in opposition to the "Third Reich". Because it was stated that the Arian did not need salvation, he dwelt at length on the "redeemed person" in large retreat courses.

He was an attentive observer of the masterly way the National Socialists made use of the psychology of the masses. He acknowledged that the Nazis knew how to initiate powerfully vital trends, and to awaken fiery enthusiasm in the youth. After a description of the decisive rôle of marriage in the divine strategy, he said, "Something like a storm must rage through the country, a storm of holy commitment to the renewal of our families. (...) What a fervour is hidden in National Socialism! We should be gripped in a similar way, otherwise we will not be able to carry out our task." Under the pressure of increasing difficulties and problems, a spirit of tiredness and pessimism began to spread through many Catholic circles. Fr Kentenich referred to this when he opened a Training Course in 1934. He underlined and emphasized supernatural hope and the optimism arising from it. He did this while fully conscious of the hardships of the situation. "When we look into our present times and the future with this tremendous optimism, we do so because we Catholics believe we have a means in hand that gives us the right to uphold this profoundly optimistic attitude. This means is Mary."

For Fr Kentenich, joy is a fundmental characteristic of Christian Life, so it should also be a special mark of the Schoenstatt Family. In 1935 he conducted a long retreat course for priests on "Perfect Priestly Joy in Life". Later, in a prayer he composed in the concentration camp at Dachau, he expressly enlarged on the importance of this virtue:

"Set us alight with glowing ardour
to go with joy to all the peoples,
to fight as witness of salvation,
and lead all men to God, rejoicing."

The topic remained timely. In his encyclical letter "Evangelii nuntiandi" Pope Paul VI came to speak about it; it is necessary to preserve spiritual zeal in the

75

proclamation of the Gospel. "Even if we should have to sow in tears." We should do so with an "inner momentum that nothing and no one can halt". A lack of holy zeal for the apostolate, which shows "in tiredness, in disappointment, in taking things easy, and above all in a lack of joy and hope", paralyzes the effect of the Gospel.

Hardly had National Socialism taken its first steps – when its actual intentions were still veiled – than Fr Kentenich saw the storm approaching. With his highly developed sense for the realities of a situation, he stated as early as 1934, "We will not be attacked so much by the Party (that is, by its doctrine and its party programme), as by its power, by its brutality; and it is only possible to withstand this by a strong and disciplined life".

The father of a young teacher who was associated with Schoenstatt was a well-known political figure belonging to the Centre Party. One day the Gestapo appeared unexpectedly at his home, searched the whole house and arrested him without giving any reason. When the teacher came to Schoenstatt, Fr Kentenich asked her to tell him all the details of what had happened. He listened attentively while she did so. When she came to the end of her report, he commented, "Now we have to go to the front". The teacher had the impression that at that moment Fr Kentenich began to reckon with the possibility that he himself might one day lose his freedom.

Fr Kentenich's vigorous response to National Socialism was to initiate a pilgrims' movement among the people. From where did he get the idea? Until then Schoenstatt had clearly developed as an élite movement. Its aim was to train leaders who should work like leaven in Catholic organizations through the genuineness of their own religious lives. This is what had been laid down in the Hörde Statutes (1919). Immediately after Hitler seized power Fr Kentenich recognised the designs of the Nazi Regime to mobilise the German people as a whole; he intuitively grasped the Regime's extraordinary ability to appeal to the masses, as well as its infectious vitality that swept everyone along with it. Vox temporis, vox Dei! The voices of a time are the voice of God! The situation demanded an answer. God's plan had to be deduced from the negative elements of ''what the others were doing''. In a letter of 31 December 1933 he wrote, ''Until now we have purposely allowed the popularization of our thoughts and spirit to recede into the background. Now we have to mobilise all the forces at our disposal to preserve the people in their Christian spirit, and to deepen it. We have to take the step from being a movement of leaders to becoming a peoples' movement, without on that account neglecting the education and organization of leaders''.

He decided that 1934 should become a ''Marian Schoenstatt Year for the People''. The courses he gave in that year (which were published by Patris Verlag in 1971 under the title ''Marian Education'') developed the fundamental pedagogical and pastoral principles for a popular Catholic movement, in order to animate and strengthen the faith of the faithful. He based himself on the following thesis: ''An enlightened veneration of Mary is the great means by which to create a profound and comprehensive popular movement in the Catholic

Church." He emphasized strongly that Christianity is not only a religion for the élite, but also for the masses (and hence has to take into account that many mistakes will be made in carrying it out in practice). For this reason he took a stand on a controversy that has repeatedly appeared in the Church: Should the Church be an élite community or also a Church for the people as a whole? If one stresses the former in a one-sided way, the Church distances herself from the people; she begins to speak a complicated language, neglects to foster popular piety, and no longer has an understanding for the religious expression of the simple people. On the other hand, if in the Church spirituality, the inner life and contemplation are undervalued or even given up, openness towards the world easily becomes enslavement to it. The Church then blurs and loses her own identity. The salt loses its flavour, the light only shines out faintly, the leaven no longer penetrates the dough. Fr Kentenich maintained that the Church is universal, that is to say, it is a Church for the élite and the general public at the same time. "It follows that the future of the Church, particularly today when one mass of people confronts another, depends more than ever before not only on an élite, but also on the masses of the people. The Church is not only the Church of the perfect, but also of the weak, the nominal Catholics, the imperfect and the under-developed" (1964).

That is why he expressly insisted in 1934, "We do not only want the people belonging to the élite, we must also get hold of the masses in the movement of faith. When you hear from the other side how they are counting upon the masses, you then know that the Church must be a Church for the masses, for the people''.

When he analysed the phenomenon that kept Germany on tenter-hooks at that time, Fr Kentenich included a factor, a power, that is often doubted, ignored or avoided. By this I mean ''the power of darkness'' (cf Col. 1:13), the devil. Very early on he became intuitively aware of the presence and powerful activity of diabolical powers in National Socialism. ''We are living at a time'', he said in 1934, ''when human forces do not measure themselves against human forces; we are living at a time when diabolical forces measure themselves against divine forces''. How are you to recognise this force? If man is active and the devil is also at work, where can you draw a line between the two? It is not easy to give a precise answer to this question. However, the following is something to hold onto: if things exceed a certain limit, if things go beyond the limits of what is merely human, we are faced with a super-human factor. If this has to do with something positive or good, we may conclude that it is due to God's influence, ''whose power working in us can do infinitely more than we can ask or imagine'' (Eph. 3:20). We may assume that this ''overwhelming power comes from God and not from us'' (2 Cor. 4:7). In contrast to this, if we are faced with an unimaginably immense evil, with extraordinary cruelty, we may draw the conclusion: such a thing is not merely the result of human intention. In such an instance it is reasonable to deduce that an evil power has intervened. (As the people say: The devil's got his finger in the pie!)

This is not the place for a dissertation on demonology. Let us just recall what Vatican Council II has to say to us on the subject. "A monumental struggle against the powers of darkness pervades the whole history of man. The battle was joined from the very origins of the world and will continue until the last day, as the Lord has attested" (The Church Today, No. 37). As far as Fr Kentenich was concerned, the power of darkness is an active force with which we have to reckon all the time. Through his death and his resurrection, Christ overcame the works of the devil. Man does not need to fear the powers of evil if he is united with the victorious power of Christ. A Christian always takes into account that God and the Evil One will be at work in history. (These are the "hidden powers behind the world's events".) When he is united with Christ, the Christian will be victor over the world ("In the world you will have trouble, but be brave: I have conquered the world") (John 16:33). This also applies to Mary, the Woman who crushes the serpent (cf Gen. 3:15).

The 8 July 1935 was the twenty-fifth anniversary of Fr Kentenich's ordination. In order that as many members of the Schoenstatt Family as possible might take part in the celebration, it was transferred to 11 August. A participant describes it as follows: "The celebration of the silver jubilee of our Union Leader's ordination was really a family festival; it was so sincere, so warm! We were brothers and sisters with their spiritual father!" That morning, at 9 a.m., Fr Kentenich officiated at a solemn Holy Mass on the Pilgrims' Square behind the shrine. The big jubilee festivities had been arranged to take place in the College auditorium at 5 p.m. To start with, Fr Alex Menningen addressed a few words of welcome to Fr Kentenich, who replied gratefully. He thanked all

80

Schoenstatt's sons ("I am thinking of the dead, I am thinking of the living, I am thinking of the coming generations") for the character of genuine community life that marked the Schoenstatt Family. "The work that has been created here is equally the work of the co-operators. I am unthinkable without you. . . . You yourselves have exercised an extremely strong influence on my personal development." And he added, "The words spoken in jest just now, which repeated an answer given by one of our members at that time, are true. . . . I had said that the talks might not be passed on, and he replied, 'He got all that knowledge from us after all!' The book in which I have been reading is the book of the times, the book of life, the book of your souls. If you had not opened up your souls so unreservedly to me, most of our spiritual achievements would never have been discovered. You can't read that sort of thing in books, you can only read it from life." He also thanked our Lady for all that had come into existence in the past twenty-five years. "What has come into existence, what has developed through me, what has developed through you, has done so through our dear Mother Thrice Admirable of Schoenstatt."

The Jubilee Year 1939 was also a year of great difficulties. ("Whoever knows the family's history, knows that Jubilee Years have always been years of suffering and trial for us.") The battle had to be waged on two fronts. On the one hand there were the problems with National Socialism, because the Gestapo began to search the houses in Schoenstatt, they cross-questioned various members, confiscated goods and arrested some

81

members. On the other hand there were tensions with the Church authorities because of the so-called "special ideas" in Schoenstatt.

A bishop, who was at that time advisor to the German Bishops' Conference on dogmatic questions, came to Schoenstatt in order to study what people there understood by our Lady's presence in the shrine and her attachment to the place. He could not find a satisfactory answer, so he wanted to take Schoenstatt's case to Rome, in order that the Congregation for the Faith (at that time it was called the "Holy Office") might study the matter. The Pallottine Vicar General immediately travelled from Rome to Schoenstatt on hearing this, and asked Fr Kentenich to give up the "special ideas". Otherwise the Holy Office would intervene and that would mean unpleasantness and loss of prestige for the whole Pallottine Society. In reply Fr Kentenich told him, "I would rather ask you first to study what we are aiming at". The superiors took up this suggestion and that ended the matter. One of the problematic "special ideas" was the "contract" or "covenant" with Mary. This referred to a "mutual contract" between Schoenstatt, God and our Lady. The representative of the bishops was of the opinion that one could not use such terms. However, when someone explained to him that it did not refer to a mutual "legal contract", but to a "free and mutual act of choice and self-surrender", and that this concept was rooted in the age-old tradition of the Marian Sodalities, the problem was solved. Nevertheless Fr Kentenich suggested that in future they should no longer speak of a "mutual contract", but of a "covenant of love". This gave rise to an important vital trend that was to strengthen the Family inwardly and prepare it for the approaching hours of trial.

Once again Fr Kentenich had interpreted the storms raging around him correctly. Even when the winds blew unpleasantly into his face, they nevertheless gave him the direction for the march into the future. Four years later, when Fr Kentenich asked himself at the outbreak of World War II what God could want of the family, he referred back to the battles of the past. He asked himself which of Schoenstatt's ideas and structures had been most hotly contested in Catholic circles. What did he do in order to discover God's will? "We take as our starting point the thought that God has allowed such hostile acts in order to draw our attention to things he wants us to stress particularly, and which he wants us to render particularly effective." In a letter for 18 October 1939 (which is known in the Schoenstatt Family as the "Second Founding Document"), Fr Kentenich summarised his answer to the current challenges in a triple imperative. The main battle had concentrated on the so-called "special ideas", in particular on the "awareness of having received a divine mission and of being God's instrument" (hence the imperative to foster with great love this awareness of having received a divine mission and of being God's instrument); then the "mutual contract and local attachment" (hence the challenge to uphold our Marian character unshakably); and, finally, the "capital of grace of the Mother Thrice Admirable of Schoenstatt" (hence the imperative to place the contributions to the capital of grace in the foreground again).

By the end of the 1930's Fr Kentenich was one of the

most esteemed priests in Germany. His fame was to a large extent the result of the popularity of his retreat courses for the clergy. It is remarkable to see how many priests came to Schoenstatt despite the difficulties caused by the persecution of the Church (in 1936 a total of 915 priests attended sixteen retreat courses; in 1937, 885 priests attended fourteen courses; in 1939, 886 attended fourteen courses; in 1940, 1 020 priests attended fifteen courses). Fr Kentenich's apostolic activity was not limited to Schoenstatt as such. He felt urged to offer his services to the whole Church in Germany, particularly in view of the critical position of the Church in relation to the National Socialist Regime. On one occasion he was with several priests in Vienna. Suddenly someone asked him for his opinion of National Socialism. He answered quite spontaneously and was amazed at the positive response of the group around him. At that moment he came to a decision: "You will now travel to every city in Germany and try to bring about similar clarity there." This lightning reaction was quite typical. There were times when he could make an important decision in a matter of seconds. But it could also happen that he could wait for weeks, months, or even years, until Divine Providence had revealed his plans more clearly to him.

As a result he travelled to Berlin, Breslau, Münster (where he spoke for four hours without pause), and other cities. He had to leave rapidly each time, "because, as soon as I had spoken, I naturally had to fear that the Gestapo would arrive. That was why I had to set off again very quickly." In the years in which he conducted the retreat courses, it was not a rare occurrence for one of his trusted followers to place a warning slip on his podium, "Beware, the enemy is listening in!" And in fact the Gestapo were keeping a closer watch and tighter control on Schoenstatt. (There is a special report of the State Security Service about Schoenstatt dated 1935, and a secret report of the Fulda Gestapo of 1939.) In order to camouflage itself as well as possible, Schoenstatt no longer called itself the "Apostolic Movement", but "A Marian Community for Prayer and Sacrifice". Since he counted on the possibility that the Gestapo would search the houses in Schoenstatt, Fr Kentenich decided to have certain archive documents burnt, while other important documents were stored away in safety at different places in Germany. The times became even harder. Fr Kentenich's central message in all its variations remained the same: to educate a new man, who is able to remain inwardly and outwardly steadfast before the approaching storms ("... for that the onward-storming era is too convulsed, uncannily relentless and opposed to God ..." he wrote in 1939). In this year, when the Second World War broke out, he conducted a retreat course for the Sisters of Mary on "Being a Child before God". The attitude of childlikeness (which is in no way childishness or infantalism), childlike heroism, should be the price paid for the conquest of inner freedom and for overcoming insecurity and anxiety. He repeated this message to priests in the two years that followed. In 1941 he conducted a series of retreat courses on the theme: "The Apocalyptic Priest". In them he attempted to give a prophetic interpretation of the events that had broken in on Europe. In the light of the Book of St John's Revelation he stated: we are living through Apocalyptic times.

(Which does not mean counting upon the end of the world. "Apocalyptic" means instead, that the present era bears a remarkable resemblance to what will happen at the end of time.) These are times in which the "powers of darkness" can almost be tangibly felt; times, therefore, in which one may hope for a special revelation of Christ's power and ultimately for his great victory. For the faithful, however, they are also times of severe trials in faith and in faithfulness.

Schoenstatt, 14 September 1941. Fr Kentenich had just started a retreat course for a hundred priests who had come from every part of Germany. In the course of the afternoon two Gestapo officials arrived and asked to speak to him. They told him to present himself the following day at the Gestapo headquarters in Coblenz. He pointed out that he had just started a retreat course for priests from all over the country, so his sudden disappearance would spread like wildfire. This argument impressed the officials, who then asked him to present himself after the course on Saturday morning, the 20th. The topic of this course was "The Marian Priest". Fr Kentenich was not in the least upset by what could happen a few days later. He was inwardly prepared for it, and none of the priests noticed in any way that their retreat master was in a dramatic situation. However, his closing words on 19 September spoke volumes: "I am now singing my Swan Song, the last hymn I shall sing in praise of our Lady ... And every praise of Mary is praise of God and praise of Christ." After dwelling on the inseparable union between Christ and Mary in God's plan and the demands of the hour, he closed with the words, "Yes, our Lady will care for us, even if what she has in store for us may outwardly seem hard. Let us be ready to die. But now we have to strive seriously in everyday life. Not to play with words, but to show by our deeds that we belong wholly to her, that we have died to ourselves and the world. We must practise dying by remaining disciplined. We don't have much time for argumentation. Today we have to act... As the disciples of our Lady we remain courageous and firm, and bravely enter into battle. Let us allow her words to us to resound constantly in our ears:

This is the instrument I have chosen,
I shall never abandon it, I swear to God!''

8. IMPRISONMENT

Schoenstatt, Saturday, 20 September 1941. In the early morning hours, before daybreak, Fr Kentenich celebrated Holy Mass in the shrine. After he had tidied up his room, he put on his oldest soutane and a pair of worn-out shoes, took leave of those who were with him, and went all alone to Coblenz, seven kilometers away. Shortly before eight he opened the front door of No. 1 in the street known as "Im Vogelsang", at that time the Gestapo headquarters. They had told him to appear at that time and he was punctually on the spot. But they didn't deal with him immediately. Using age-old tactics of wearing people down they let him wait till 1 p.m. Only then did they begin to question him. He was accused of speaking against the State and the Nazi ideology. In order to prove his hostile attitude to the people they read him extracts from talks he had given ("We'll keep to our cross, even if the others keep to their cross." "Germany must do penance and make reparation for all the dirt." "My life-task consists in showing up National Socialism.") Fr Kentenich shrugged off the accusations. He remained calm. ("I always remained calm. I had battled everything through beforehand, because I knew how they usually did things. So I could cope inwardly with everything.") He decisively rejected the accusation that he betrayed his people and his Fatherland. He did not, so he said, identify the German people with the Party that was just then in power. In order to show how much he loved his Fatherland, he quoted the talk he had given on 18 October 1914, in which he had encouraged his young audience to make full use of the great war in Europe as an extraordinarily favourable means to further their self-education, and in this way to free their Fatherland from overpowering enemies and place it at the head of the ancient world. However, no arguments carried any weight, and truth did not count at that moment. The decision had already been taken. "Yes, we will have to keep you here," the Gestapo official told him. "I have to conduct a retreat in München, and if I don't turn up, the fact of my arrest will be known throughout southern Germany." "We will have to inform them that you cannot conduct this course." With that he was led downstairs to a single cell in the cellars (formerly a bank vault). Fr Kentenich commented not without humour to the official who led the way, "At long last I can have a holiday for once". The place where they took him was not particularly suitable for that purpose: the floor, walls and ceiling were concrete, there was no heating, the ventilation was poor. (For this reason he repeatedly caught a cold and his nose bled frequently.) Fr Kentenich asked to be re-examined, and this was granted. It took place the following Sunday. He tried to prove that one of the questions that had been read out to him, and for which he stood accused, was not authentic; he could never have said such a thing. The Gestapo were used to meeting with a subservient attitude in their prisoners, so they were very surprised at this prisoner. "I stand before you as a lawyer," he said. To which they replied, "Alright, but you are an imprisoned lawyer". He was led down to his cell again, the "bunker". That was the name given to the place where the real criminals were imprisoned. From the neighbouring cells came cries

"Carissime Confrater! Since people later like to exalt 'Letters from Prison' by placing them with the acts of martyrs, I hesitate to write. In the end, however, I have to do so if you are not to remain without any news about me. So as briefly as possible a few notes. Tell everyone who is interested that I am well. In the first four weeks I could pray with the Creed: descended into the underworld; since 18 October, however, 'ascended into heaven', i.e., to higher heights where I lead the contemplative life of a Carmelite monk. Body and soul quickly adapted to the change. All in all, no reason for the creation of legends and tales of horror." In conclusion he wrote, "Whoever is looking for me and wants to visit me will find me at any time in the heart of God and our Lady. All who have inscribed themselves into these hearts are constantly with me. So conversation is not lacking. Now I have come to the end of my wisdom. One thing more: I may not forget it. Many thanks to all who take so much trouble over my laundry. May the words of the beatitude come true for them: Blessed are the merciful, for they shall receive mercy." The way Fr Kentenich had mastered the four weeks in the bunker made a deep impression not only in the prison, but even on the people from the Gestapo. Besides this we have his own confession, "Down in the bunker I did not have a single bitter second". Without having done anything on his part to achieve it, he became a well-known figure in the prison, even the warders greeted him. When the occupants of cells were changed he became the neighbour of Fr Eise (one of his co-operators in Schoenstatt, who had also been arrested). "I immediately made my identity known by knocking. We conversed by means of all sorts of signs and entertained ourselves in our own way. We also sang a great deal together: 'Unconquered we shall remain' (closing line of the hymn of the Schoenstatt Family).''

The rainy season had started. Each day the prisoners were given a time for exercise in the prison courtyard. Since Fr Kentenich had taken his oldest shoes, which had holes in them, to Coblenz, the water came in at various places. His feet were often wet. One day, towards the end of October, he asked one of the warders (later known as the ''small messenger'') whether he could not pass St Joseph's Hospital (which was staffed by Sisters of Mary), and ask the superior to send him a good pair of shoes. He wrote a brief message to this effect. ''On Friday or Saturday could someone bring me shoes with my laundry from Schoenstatt. Those I have here leak…'' The warder said he was ready to take over the messenger service. Together with the shoes he brought a note from the superior – the first illegal contact had been made. From that time onward two warders kept Fr Kentenich in illegal contact with Schoenstatt. The one was a Protestant; because of his size he was called ''the big messenger''. It was Fr Kentenich's conviction that he had to make use of all available means in order to serve the Schoenstatt Family, despite the risk this included. (''To start with the two messengers brought only a few notes along, but it didn't take long before I began to receive whole bundles of letters; I became ever more daring, but it was very dangerous.'')

Via the two messengers the sisters sent all that was necessary for the celebration of Holy Mass. This was strictly forbidden. One day ''the big messenger'' offered to bring everything – hosts, wine, a tiny chalice and a small missal. Fr Kentenich hid them behind a few books on the table, which stood exactly opposite the peephole in the door. "I celebrated Holy Mass very early in the morning," he related later, "when activity was at its height, because the cells were being cleaned. People were shouting right through the house. The doors were unlocked, the warders came into the cells. Keys rattled, the doors flew open, buckets were carried out, beds were made, cells swept. While the others were running around, I said Holy Mass. I placed the vessels quite openly on the table. If a check was made, I quickly put everything away." It is remarkable how much calm and daring Fr Kentenich showed in prison. The question involuntarily arises: What was the source of this attitude? He himself gives us an answer in one of his letters: "You, and all who form their lives by the blank cheque and Inscriptio – of this I am convinced – would find it just as easy as I do." It was said in the prison that of the eighty-five priests who had passed through in the previous year, 99% had left it as embittered and inwardly broken men. One of the prisoners who was unable to cope with the situation once had an opportunity to be with Fr Kentenich and asked him if he hadn't found it hard at times. "I haven't had a hard hour, no, not even a hard second, and that includes the time I was imprisoned in the cellar, which is an extraordinary method to wear one down," was the answer.

The priest could hardly believe his ears. And yet those were not empty words, they were the simple reality. Fr Kentenich had prepared himself for a long time for such circumstances. (" ... the reason for this is that I have allowed myself to be borne for a very long time on the wings of longing to what I have experienced and to much worse. So I seemed to myself to be like a wanderer who after a long wait has finally reached the land of his longing and silent dreams.'') We are concerned here with a life that was radically and totally at the disposal of God's will as it is made known through any given situation. It is what St Ignatius Loyola called ''holy indifference''. If you consider the natural opposition of human nature to suffering, it is normally very difficult, if not quite impossible, to reach this ''holy indifference'', unless you consciously aim at love for the cross. This attitude has come to be called the Inscriptio by the Schoenstatt Family. In the sense used by Fr Kentenich it may be described as follows: ''One often says to God: You may send me anything, only not that! Inscriptio consists in saying to God: You can really send me anything, but in particular and very concretely just that which I fear. Such an attitude presupposes radical trust in God as our Father, who would never send a cross or suffering without at the same time giving us the strength to bear it. Christianity is not a religion of suffering, nor is the measure of suffering synonymous with perfection. The suffering foreseen for us by the Father can only be a sign of perfection to the extent that it is borne patiently and transformed into love.'' From his cell Fr Kentenich conducted an intensive correspondence with the Schoenstatt Family. Because this was illegal, he constantly risked his life. The extraordinary trials he was undergoing, meant at the same time the granting of extraordinary graces and much inner light. ''At that time my mind was so full of light,'' he remarked, ''that I had only to read it off. ... It was like this: When I got up in the morning I wrote down what had been bathed in light in me during the night." He wrote down meditations on the situation of the Family, the Church and the world. Europe, indeed the whole world, was in flames, it was exposed to the destruction of the Second World War. Fr Kentenich tried to penetrate the darkness of the times and to anticipate the future: "On the horizon, slowly becoming clearly recognizable, there appear the great structural lines of a new world order; an old world is being burnt up." In the first days of 1942 Fr Kentenich sent the Sisters of Mary in Schoenstatt a work that he "had written under most primitive conditions and without reference works". It was a study on the love of Christ, and bore the title: "Nova Creatura in Jesu et Maria". He had written it with a pencil on paper used for making paper bags and without the support of a table. His intention was to introduce the Family more deeply into love for Christ. ("I do not want to die before the Family has seen its ideal of Christ clearly and has embraced it whole-heartedly in the individual members.") He had always taught that Mary leads to Christ, that the two form an inseparable two-in-oneness in God's plan; that a Family with a strongly Marian character must distinguish itself by a great and deep love for Christ, the Lord.

He summarised his desire in a prayer he composed at that time: "Lord, if you do not consider *me* worthy of proclaiming you to your loved ones, then let your Mother prevail upon you to choose another instrument. I shall then at least give you my health, strength and life in the background for this God-like gift. Do not allow your Family to be tossed about by severe storms until it knows

95

and loves you better. Mother, it is true, until now you have led your children to our Lord, but if you are to continue and complete your activity you require our conscious, comprehensive and penetrating co-operation. Do not allow your own to put out on the high seas before they have completed this work to some extent through your instruments. I am at your disposal for this purpose with all that I am and have.

Do you want my work: Adsum! (Here I am!)

Do you want all my intellectual powers to bleed slowly to death: Adsum!

Do you want my death: Adsum!

But see to it that everyone you have given me may love our Lord, and learn to live and die for him.''

On 13 January 1942 Fr Kentenich was again questioned by the Gestapo. Because he did not give them the answers they expected and wanted, they threatened to send him to the concentration camp. On 16 January he was given a medical examination to see whether he was fit for camp life. This examination was very superficial, his heart and lungs were not considered at all. Despite his delicate health he was certified fit for camp life. A handwritten notification reached Schoenstatt the following day. ''I have just been examined to see whether I am fit for camp life. Result: Fit! Now, no one may worry about me.'' From that moment on the leaders in Schoenstatt made use of every possible means in their power to prevent Fr Kentenich being sent to Dachau. They managed to get the doctor who had examined him to agree to a re-examination, although one condition had to be fulfilled, Fr Kentenich had to apply for this in writing. In this case the doctor was prepared to reverse his medical finding. Fr Kentenich had to face a difficult decision: Should he make the application or not? What did God want of him? On 19 January he wrote: "Thank you for your efforts with the doctor. Please do not take it amiss if I do not continue to spin the thread you have drawn." Those were hard days and hours. "I did not find it easy to battle through to this decision; because to go to Dachau means going to certain death and separating myself from the whole Family." Fr Kentenich was given no inner clarity on what God wanted of him, and the decision he had to make was a momentous one. Should he freely take the step that led to the concentration camp? Was he allowed to jeopardize his whole work and the Family? And if the separation was forever – through his death – was he allowed, in view of this possibility, to take this step of his own accord? Was that really God's will? "My restlessness over this matter gave me no peace," he related some years later. "Those were a few terribly hard days. Inwardly I battled and prayed." The decisive question was: What did God want? "I had no vision, no dream, nor even a special enlightenment. All that was left to me in this battle was simple faith in Divine Providence." It was a matter of grave concern to him whether the sisters would understand his action correctly if he turned down the doctor's offer. They had prayed and sacrificed so much for his liberation, so would they not feel that rejecting this offer was ingratitude? "Hour after hour I walked the few steps up and down my cell, battled and prayed and did not know what to do. Should I fill in the application form? I could not do it."

He spent the night between 19 and 20 January in prayer,

and struggled inwardly to recognize God's will. On the 20th, during Holy Mass, he received an answer; he felt inwardly certain what he should do: He wanted to use no human means for his liberation, but only the Schoenstatt Family's self-surrender to God through the heroic striving to live the Inscriptio. It was in this spirit that he wrote a few lines to Fr Menningen, his faithful follower: "Please understand this answer through faith in the reality of supernature and the interweaving of the destinies of the members of the family."

At first the Family did not understand his decision. All begged him to make use of the opportunity that had been offered and fill in the application. But Fr Kentenich had come to a decision. He never departed from what he had recognised as God's will. ("And now one visitor after the other comes to the tower window and makes my decision difficult. ... Now letters are also arriving. ... They martyr me... But I cannot do anything else.") In this great and heroic hour of his life he remained completely human, he felt and he suffered. "How difficult the decision was for me!" he related later. "That was one of the hardest moments of my life. ... In what a human way I felt it at that time. Tears came into my eyes at times. I was happy at the time that I wore glasses."

A few days later, when he received a positive reaction from leading circles in the Family to his decision of 20 January, he became firmly convinced that he would soon be set free and be able to return to Schoenstatt. But this did not happen. What was the meaning of the delay? What was its purpose? According to Fr Kentenich's interpretation they were being offered an opportunity to grow in the heroism of the three theological virtues –

faith, hope and love. "We now have the most favourable opportunity to dare to throw ourselves with an heroic gesture into supernature."

On 9 March Fr Kentenich began his private retreat. Through his "Information Service" he got to know that he would be transported to Dachau two days later. He immediately wrote to Schoenstatt and gave instructions: "On Wednesday we leave for Dachau ... remain simple, selfless, faithful and strong. ... I look upon the situation in this way: 1. A change of air does one good. So it is an act of special love when it is placed at your disposal. 2. The sacrifice connected with it should be a lightning-conductor for the Family. However, the latter must prepare itself for severe storms. ..." He asked the Sisters of Mary to sing the whole "Hymn of Thanksgiving" daily until he returned. "The day will come when we will see more clearly why everything happened in this way. At any rate, let us remember in every circumstance of life: We love and then everything will turn out well. God always remains generous – even if we can't understand him." On the morning of 11 March, Fr Kentenich and other prisoners were taken to Coblenz Station from where they were taken by train to Dachau.

9. DACHAU

Dachau. Only a few kilometers from München. A well-known name, but one of tarnished honour. A place of infamy: as from 1933 the National Socialists built a concentration camp there. Thirty-four barracks were built on a field bounded to the west by a large canal of water that was inaccessible from the outside, and a high-voltage electrified barbed wire fence, with watchmen in the towers and SS people with vicious dogs to guard it. It was intended that five to seven thousand prisoners should be kept there. This did not prevent the Gestapo from allowing the number of inmates in the camp to increase to almost forty thousand. People called the camp ''the hell of Dachau''. Ironically the camp's motto gave promise of freedom. (''Work makes you free'' was the inscription worked into the cast iron entrance gate to the camp.) The truth looked different – the inhabitants of the camp were condemned to live in primitive, brutal conditions that were quite unworthy of human beings. ''You have no rights here,'' yelled the camp commander to the new arrivals at the first introduction. ''The German people has kicked you out. You have only one right – to be trampled upon.'' The food was kept to such a minimum that if a prisoner had to live on what was provided he would in practice die of starvation. In the morning each prisoner received about 1/3 of a liter of coffee (in reality it was not much more than water); at midday they were given vegetables in the form of soup which contained almost no fat; and at night 1/5 or 1/7 of a loaf of bread. Whoever was able to do so would examine the pots in the hope of finding a potato or some scraps of

100

food. As a result of the lack of vitamins, many prisoners developed ulcers and cellulitis which seldom healed. Dachau not only had the name, it was in fact a "hell". It happened often enough that transport trains arrived with starving prisoners who were more dead than alive. When the SS noticed that one of the prisoners had collapsed from starvation, but was still alive, they made a sport of kicking him with their heavy boots until he was quite dead. There were terrible times of starvation. In 1942 only living corpses, not human beings, dragged themselves painfully through the camp. And in midwinter 1944, when various epidemics broke out, many prisoners were no more than skin and bone. It was not unusual to see them lying in the camp streets, and if they could still walk, the one had to support the other.

Whoever was admitted to Dachau was from then on separated from his family and home. A completely primitive life awaited him. There was hardly a green plant to be seen in the camp, no flowers, only one row of trees. On their arrival, the prisoners were taken to the admission block. They were harnessed to carts carrying SS men who drove them with whips. None of this happened by chance or was simply improvised. These actions were consciously and deliberately planned, the aim being to break the prisoner's personality and to destroy all that was noble in his character. The preparation of one of the notorious "invalid transports" – a one-way journey to the gas chambers – resembled a cattle sale. The prisoners were driven, often naked, past the SS, who then selected those they considered still able to work, the rest were condemned to death.

Dachau was a "hell". They conducted experiments on

the prisoners, people like you and me, as though they were guinea-pigs. They were for example, thrown into ice-cold water in order to see how long a person can survive such conditions. They were inoculated with bacteria and bacilli in order to study the reaction. Malaria experiments were carried out. People were simply murdered. Any gold teeth were torn out of the prisoners' mouths. And there were the highly-refined punishment drills, for example, the "Saxon greeting". The prisoner had to place his hands at the back of his neck, squat on his heels, and then hop. While in this position, a person can hardly breathe. He can bear it for a minute or two at most, then he collapses. It often happened that he was then shot dead. It was the custom to make the prisoners stand for hours or even the whole day on the parade ground. (Fr Kentenich had made it a habit to stand while he gave his talks. So he did not find it such a hardship to stand still for hours on end.) Another punishment was to place a prisoner on a chair or ladder, tie his hands with rope, which was then fastened to the branch of a tree. Then the chair or ladder was removed and the prisoner was left to hang there for an hour or longer.

On 11 March Fr Kentenich waited with other prisoners at Coblenz Station for the train with prison trucks that was to transport them to Dachau. The presence of two Sisters of Mary in their blue uniform dress, who dared to approach to a certain distance from the prisoners, gave this inhuman situation a note of humanity and compassion. Fr Kentenich's immediate companions were Fr Carls, Caritas Director, and a despairing communist who never left his side. They had to change trains at Wiesbaden, and here they were handcuffed.

Throughout the journey they were guarded by the SS with their dogs. They were given nothing to eat or drink. After two strenuous days on the way they arrived on Friday, 13 March, in Dachau. A prisoner described their arrival: "At the admission to the concentration camp, with all its formalities that took a number of hours, I witnessed how both priests (one of them Fr Kentenich) were showered with mockery and derision by the SS." When they passed through the "political section" they were photographed and given a number. Fr Kentenich received the number 29392. The head of the SS got the idea that he had to "soften up" the new arrival, who exuded so much calm and security. He insulted him grossly and put all sorts of questions to him. When he received no answer – Fr Kentenich only looked at him calmly and smiled in a friendly way – he lost his temper and threatened to hit Fr Kentenich, but he did not do so. A few days later the two met again in the office where particulars about each prisoner were recorded. The officer recognised Fr Kentenich again immediately. "The missionary can clean my bicycle," he said. "Yes, I can do that for you," answered Fr Kentenich, "but not because I am forced. I want to do you a service as a free person." "No ... you needn't do it," the officer replied. While he wrote down Fr Kentenich's particulars, Fr Kentenich asked him why he had shouted at him like that the day before. "Everything is tried out to make people afraid," was the answer. Then this commanding officer took Fr Kentenich into his office and told him his life story. After his arrival in the camp, Fr Kentenich was sent to the admission block in the ordinary way. There he immediately won the confidence of the Block Senior,

Hugo Gutmann, a communist. Fr Kentenich soon began to work for the priests. Although all religious activity was forbidden, he gave a short talk every evening; he continued to do so for a long time until it became impossible. However he always found opportunities to speak to smaller groups. "We owe Fr Kentenich a great debt of gratitude," Fr Hans Carls, Caritas Director from Wuppertal, later stated, "because each evening he gave us points for meditation. He did so either on the block street, or later in a corner of the dormitory". Another of his activities was to distribute Holy Communion secretly to his confrères. He received consecrated hosts clandestinely almost every day.

The prisoners were allowed to write a short letter every two weeks. Fr Kentenich made use of this opportunity on 22 March and sent his first brief letter to Schoenstatt. "I am sure you have been awaiting my first letter from my new home for some time. So I am making use of the first opportunity to fulfil your wish. How am I? Paul would answer: 'I can do all things in Him who strengthens me.' I am alright. And what else? For the rest I am constantly in spirit with my loved ones, and hope to be able to serve you more than before. When the second Fall became a reality, and our Lord decided to fulfil the Father's wish and take on himself suffering and death, he spoke those memorable words: 'The grain of wheat must first be buried in the ground and die, then it will yield much fruit.' I think the same. And you, the whole Family, are striving to take your total self-surrender seriously. To all, up and down, greetings, J Kentenich."

The prisoner made no complaints, there was no trace of depression. His words reveal a deepened attitude of obedience to God the Father and heroic self-surrender for his followers.

Hundreds of people died of the general starvation in those months. Emaciated and totally exhausted, the prisoners easily fell victim to epidemics and other sicknesses. Fr Kentenich felt the first signs of dysentery. He wrote later: "The first signs of the sickness also appeared in me, but in the end everything always went well again. In the end I was no more than a skeleton." Nevertheless, he always gave a portion of the little food he received to someone else.

It was a crisis situation. Together with the other Schoenstatt members in Dachau, Fr Kentenich elected our Lady the Queen of the Camp and the "Mother who provides Bread" on 2 July. They promised for their part to live the Inscriptio attitude, that is, to free themselves from every attachment to what is earthly, to surrender themselves completely to God's will, and to be generous in giving, trusting in the admonition of the Gospel: "Give and it will be given to you." Despite this critical situation, Fr Kentenich developed intense mental and spiritual activity. "At that time," he related later, "I had tremendous powers of concentration and I was always spiritually alert. When compared with my physical weakness and the starvation, and the immanence of death by starvation, I possessed an extremely strong spiritual and intellectual vitality. I was constantly holding courses and calling the prisoners in the block together."

The 24 June was a most dangerous day. Fr Kentenich's

name could have appeared on the list for "transport", which meant certain death. The Block Senior suddenly sent for him and told him that a commission had come from Berlin to inspect the camp, and those who were not attached to some working commando were in danger of being sent on "transport". The communist acted quickly. He took Fr Kentenich to another block and gave him another name and number. In this way he was able to avert the danger and save Fr Kentenich's life.

On 16 July 1942 Fr Kentenich took a step that has profoundly influenced the Schoenstatt Family. He did so in two highly secret celebrations that followed each other on that day. Together with Dr Fritz Kühr, a well-known sociologist and politician belonging to the Centre Party, he founded the core community of the Schoenstatt Family Movement. He had now reached a goal he had long had in mind and for which he had been looking for a favourable opportunity, or, we would do better to say, for a suitable instrument. And together with a lawyer from Austria, Dr Edi Pesendörfer, he called the community of the Schoenstatt Brothers of Mary into existence. The two then began the time of their novitiate in the midst of the concentration camp. Their novice master was naturally no one else than Fr Kentenich; it took great daring to carry out this task. He related later, "I went to them at great risk to my own life and climbed through the window. I had to take into account that I might be shot down while doing it. The guards were standing about everywhere with loaded rifles. But our Lady always protected me".

At the end of August Fr Kentenich was transferred from the admission block to Block 28, which was occupied by

Polish priests. Between 1939 and 1945, 2 720 priests from twenty-five or more nations passed through the camp. Of these 1 777 were Poles; 858 of them died in the camp. Since Fr Kentenich knew no Polish, he conversed with the priests in Latin, and they were soon on good terms. "That was very good for me," he explained later. "I got to know the Polish soul. They are a mercurial people." This liking was mutual. One Pole recalls him in these words, "His priestly attitude was admirable. He held religious conferences for us Polish priests, basing his talks on the Apocalypse of St John. I can well remember that we all listened to him with great interest. In every sentence one could feel that this was a priest with a deep inner life." Two months later he was transferred again, this time to Block 26, where the German priests were kept. Even from there he remained in contact with his Polish confrères. He arranged for them to receive wine and hosts so that they could celebrate the Eucharist.

Towards the end of this year, at the beginning of winter, a typhus epidemic broke out in the camp. Hundreds of prisoners, even some from the priests' block, died. The camp administration put the whole camp into quarantine from 25 January to 14 March. On 2 February 1943 Fr Kentenich dictated the "Hymn of the Home". It was addressed to the Sisters of Mary in the "Exerzitienhaus" in Schoenstatt, which had the ideal to be a "Sunny House". It is a fundamental text in which Schoenstatt's ideals find classic expression. It is a hymn that is full of light, which originated in the dark night of Dachau. In its six verses it sings of Schoenstatt as our "Homeland", the "land so homely, warm, a land built by Eternal Love"; "a land so rich and pure, reflecting God's own beauty''; the ''land which is like heaven, the longed-for realm where freedom reigns''; the ''land where joy prevails, where people live in calm contentment, since they possess eternal riches''; ''the land where truthfulness, justice and love reign''; the ''land prepared to fight, where victory is always won''. Each verse begins: ''Do you know the land …?'' and the refrain answers, ''This wonderland is known to me … where our Thrice Admirable Mother reigns, surrounded by the children she loves most … it is the land called home, my Schoenstatt land''.

The Sisters had asked him to write them a text they could frame and display. He decided to answer their request in the form of a poem. He immediately began dictating it. When it was finished in January 1944, it had grown to be 5 870 verses. In this didactic poem he touched upon the most varied topics (theological, philosophical, pedagogical, ascetical and pastoral) which were of interest to the leaders of the Sisters of Mary. He called this work ''The Shepherd's Mirror'', and this study alone (not counting the other works he wrote) would justify the statement he made later, ''I dictated a whole library in Dachau''. Fr Dresbach served as secretary, and he recalls, ''Fr Kentenich dictated very fluently without once laying down the comprehensive disposition in writing''.

While he did this a change in strategy matured in Fr Kentenich. Almost a year had passed since his arrival in the camp. Until then he had devoted himself in princi-ple to the priests and had tried to create a community with them. Every second week he had made use of the opportunity available to every prisoner and had written to Schoenstatt. By using quotations from the Bible and biblical names he was able to give the Family, in particular the Sisters of Mary, veiled instructions. In the meantime, however, he had found out that none of his letters after the end of October 1942 had reached Schoenstatt. What had happened?

At the beginning of November the Gestapo had searched one of the houses in Schoenstatt and had found a collection of Fr Kentenich's letters from Dachau in the room of Lotte Holubars, a teacher, and a member of the Institute of Our Lady of Schoenstatt. Anyone reading the letters individually would not have had any grounds for suspicion. But a collection that had been duplicated was without doubt bound to arouse the suspicion of the Gestapo. As from November, Fr Kentenich's letters were confiscated by the censor in the concentration camp and sent to the Coblenz Gestapo. The same thing was done with his New Year's letter. On realising this, Fr Kentenich decided not to use the legal channels any more to write to Schoenstatt. But what could he do instead? Should he give up letter contact? Should he make use of illegal channels? While he thought over these questions he made a novena in preparation for 25 March, the feast of the Annunciation of the Lord to Mary. On this day he took two far-reaching decisions: 1. in future he would devote himself entirely to building up Schoenstatt in the camp; 2. he would be on the look out for ways that would enable him to take the direction of the Family outside the camp more vigorously in hand. Slowly and purposefully he made use of the possibilities that offered themselves, and as time went by he built up a whole network of communication channels through which he kept in close touch with Schoenstatt. A Polish priest offered to smuggle post out of the camp for him through a trusted agent. One of his collaborators, Fr Fischer, was appointed to a new working commando and was sent to the greenhouse. There civilians from Dachau worked shoulder to shoulder with the hundreds of prisoners, and so new contacts arose. Shortly afterwards another possibility opened up: it became possible to arrange visits from relatives during the working hours in the greenhouse. As a result, two Sisters of Mary managed to visit Dachau four times that year and take up direct contact with the concentration camp. Meanwhile Fr Kentenich was working in the disinfection commando. It was his task to mend the straw sacks and bolsters. After he had made the decision of 25 March, he was inwardly certain that God did not want him to work for the concentration camp, but solely for the Schoenstatt Family. Divine Providence arranged that the leader of his working group, Jakob Koch, protected him, and that Fathers Dresbach and Ludwig Bettendorf, both Schoenstatt members, the latter a parish priest of the diocese of Treves, could act as his secretaries. Fr Kentenich wrote not a single letter after January, but now he began to dictate. In the months to come he was to dictate hundreds, indeed thousands of letters. This meant playing constantly with his life. In Dachau no one was allowed to possess even a slip of paper that did not bear the official stamp. An example: a worker once tried to write a few harmless things home through illegal channels. He was found out and was sent on transport to the gas chambers. How was Fr Kentenich to receive answers from outside? The problem was solved in the following way: People he trusted worked in the camp post office. Every in-coming parcel had to be examined; an exception was made for small parcels and for whatever came by express post. Fr Kentenich immediately informed those outside how they should pack the parcels. From then on he received a small parcel every fortnight – it was full of letters. This was dangerous. Besides, it was a problem to read all the letters. "I read them at top speed," he related later. "My eyes watered as a result. I did not cry because of the touching contents, but rather because my eyes were really strained by all the reading." Even so he could not read all the letters and they began to pile up. What was he to do? Because Fr Kentenich was supposed to be mending bolsters, he turned one of them into a bag in which he could hide the letters. On the one side he stored those he had read, and on the other the ones he still had to read. Years later he related, "I did nothing else than sew up and open this huge letter bag again and again; I read and worked for myself. If someone came we were always busily at work. My letters always lay in front of me."

On the whole things went well. Sometimes, however, the situation became dangerous. One day while they were at work one of the worst SS men remained to watch them. Fr Kentenich quickly threw his bolster to one side. "Put that bolster back where it was," shouted the SS man. Fr Kentenich obeyed, but he took another bolster that did not contain letters and placed it where the first had been. "That is not the bolster you had. I shall come and examine it immediately!" But he did not arrive.

. . . Writing illegal letters endangered the lives of the other occupants of the priests' block, because if it were discovered, the whole block could be severely punished. Fr Kentenich had two or three priests to whom he dictated (''the cheekier the better!'') In order to protect himself he had come to an agreement with an Italian priest that in the event of an unexpected inspection, he would throw his bolster onto the Italian's bed (because no one would be suspicious of the Italian, since he never received anything).

Fr Kentenich did not always receive just small parcels. In March 1943, shortly before Easter, he received a big parcel containing two cakes. Fr Fischer remarked that he would personally have to investigate what they were like. ''He wouldn't eat them all up, but only just have a taste,'' remarked Fr Kentenich jokingly and gave one cake to another prisoner, Joseph Joos. Soon afterwards he returned the gift. Outwardly it was a lovely cake, but inside it was another story – it was a diary! Once again Fr Kentenich had to read it at top speed.

In comparison to 1942, the year 1943 was more peaceful. Nevertheless dangerous situations arose from time to time. A week before Christmas a ticklish episode occurred on the camp square between Fr Kentenich and the camp Commandant von Redwitz. While they were mustered for counting, the Commandant, who was very drunk, approached the block of German priests and turned to Fr Kentenich, who was standing in the fourth or fifth row. ''Hey, you Spiritual Advisor . . . are you really a Spiritual Advisor?'' ''No,'' replied Fr Kentenich, ''I am not a Spiritual Advisor, but I do at times give spiritual advice.'' ''What?'' yelled von Redwitz in a rage, because he thought Fr Kentenich had made the play on words as a personal dig, ''you want to give me,

112

the camp Commandant, spiritual advice, you, rogue, you! I'll show you . . . '' Fr Kentenich had to report to the camp Commandant the following day, but the episode fortunately had no negative repercussions.

The war continued. The Resistance Movement grew in the territories occupied by Germany, and the groups of prisoners coming to Dachau grew in number. The over-crowding was so bad that it was almost unbearable. Then came an infestation of lice, the worst that had occurred in the camp. On 9 March 1944 Fr Kentenich and two other priests were shut up in the examination bunker. They had to appear the following day before a high-ranking commission of SS and Gestapo. It had come from Berlin with the expressed commission to cross-question Fr Kentenich. He was accused of various crimes, among others, that he carried on illegal correspondence. In reply to the latter accusation, the prisoner stated that after he had written his last official letter on 9 January 1943, he had not written another letter – either legal-ly or illegally. He said this with the conviction of one speaking the truth. And in fact he had written nothing. (What he didn't tell them – and why should he? – was that he had dictated instead.) After this examination he was allowed to return to the priests' block. On arrival he said to Fr Dresbach as though nothing had happened: ''We shall go on writing this afternoon!''

In the spring of 1944 (between April and June) he dic-tated ''The Marian Instrument's Piety'', a fundamen-tal work in Schoenstatt's spirituality. On instructions from the Berlin commission, the camp administration separated the German from the non-German priests. The former occupied Room 2 and 3 of Block 26. Fr

Kentenich had to go to Room 3 where 230 men were incarcerated together. They slept in three-tier bunk beds. This meant that he no longer had the table of Room 4 at his disposal. They had to work with greater care. The above-mentioned study ends with the "Instrument's Hymn", one verse of which runs as follows:

"Threats of Satan and the world,
stormy weather may surround us,
you will conquer every need,
your omnipotence goes with us.
Our safe refuge is your heart,
giv'n to us as heaven's gate."

At the end of May 1943 a number of groups had formed among the priests in the concentration camp. They were divided into two circles: two groups for leaders (the "Hand Circle" and the "Heart Circle") and five League groups. Their membership was drawn from priests from Poland, Czechoslovakia, Italy, France, Belgium, Holland and Germany. What united them was their common love for our Lady and their readiness to be her willing instruments in the service of the Church. Caring for these groups was additional work and exertion for Fr Kentenich. Since every form of organized gathering was forbidden in the camp, he usually spoke to each group individually. This meant that he sometimes had up to five group meetings in one evening. It was autumn, and the rains had started. On the whole the meetings took place in the open. It was not unusual to see Fr Kentenich moving from one group to the next with his clothes soaked through and through. He never allowed bad weather to daunt him. He kept up these evening talks until his release in April 1945. Besides this he inspired his confrères to set aside the first Sunday of every month as a day of recollection. His work with the priests reached a climax on 18 October 1944, the thirtieth anniversary of Schoenstatt's foundation. It was raining. In the talk he gave to priests from a number of nations he said, among other things, "Until now the work has been limited. It is now breaking through this barrier and is becoming international." How did he come to take this daring step of founding an "International" in the concentration camp? The answer is simple: Through the intuition that had accompanied him like a radar apparatus, as it were, and that was to go with him in the future as well – practical faith in Divine Providence. He was aware that he was the founder of a work with universal dimensions. Priests from many nations belonged to it. ... God spoke through circumstances. Two months later, on 8 December, he enlarged on this idea. He took as his starting point a saying that is applied to the Apostle Paul: "Cor Pauli, cor mundi", that is, "Paul's heart embraced the whole world with its love". Our hearts, which are all too often made small by egoism, should be like Mary's heart, like Christ's heart, like God's heart. "Our heart belongs to all people, to all nations, no matter what their name and whatever history they may have had."

This international direction and strategy is openly displayed in a prayer Fr Kentenich composed especially for the occasion:

"From all the nations gathered here and suff'ring
select the best to serve and spread your kingdom;

accept them as your instruments and use them
to re-direct the peoples to the Saviour;
let Schoenstatt spread and bear rich fruit throughout
   the world
to honour you and glorify the Trinity.''

The last verse shows the direction he intended to take
once the war and Dachau were behind him:
"Let us appoint you this world's Queen and
   Sovereign,
our hearts aflame with ardent love and longing
to set the world on fire for your service,
that all the peoples may reach home in safety.
Your holy heart is this world's surest port of peace,
the sign of God's election and the gate to heaven.''

Outside the camp the war continued. Gradually it
became evident that Germany would be defeated. Stauf-
fenberg's attempt to do away with Hitler failed. The last
months of the war were to bring indescribable suffering
upon the German people. The cities and important
strategic points in Germany were destroyed during the
night air raids. In the middle of November Fr Fischer
received a letter from his sister, Catherine, who described
the brutal destruction of Coblenz in the bombing. Fr
Kentenich listened silently as the letter was read to him
and afterwards composed a prayer which he gave to Fr
Fischer the following day for his sister. In it we read:

"I trust you fully
and am but seeking
to do uprightly
the Father's bidding

though judgement day
may come on us.
For he will lead me
through every darkness
despite confusion,
he'll lead me homewards
at your kind hand
to our Fatherland.''

The last months of the concentration camp were chaotic.
The destruction of all the means of production and the
communications network resulted in the return of starvation conditions for the prisoners. Besides this, towards
the end of 1944, an epidemic of typhus broke out. A
large number of prisoners died every day. In January
1945 around three thousand died; in February and
March the numbers rose to about four thousand. Fr
Kentenich, who was receiving parcels, did what he
possibly could to help others, in particular the most
needy. He felt intuitively that his stay in the camp was
coming to an end.

Early in 1945, Himmler, the head of the SS and of concentration camps, secretly tried to negotiate an armistice.
In order to show his good will, he released priests from
the concentration camp at Dachau. On 2 April, Easter
Monday, Fr Kentenich held the monthly recollection day
for the Schoenstatt members under the motto: ''Pro-
cedamus in pace, in nomine Domini et Dominae Matris
ter Admirabilis!'' – Let us go forth in peace in the name
of our Lord and our Lady, the Mother Thrice Admirable!'' On 6 April, towards 9 a.m., he left Dachau.
Those words still stood blazoned over the entrance gate:

"Work makes you free!" He left Dachau a free and un-broken man. He owed this, however, not so much to work (although he had been extraordinarily active), as to God. "I left the camp so completely healthy in body and soul because God had given me an extraordinary degree of inner freedom." Dachau had set the seal on the divine character of the work he had founded. And an admonition for the future: "I am convinced that the concentration camps were the preparatory camps; the whole world would later have been governed as they were."

By the end of the war in May 1945 Germany's towns and cities with their industrial centres lay in ruins. The means of production and the communications network had been destroyed by the Allies in their bombing raids. The Russians occupied the Eastern part of the country, the English the North, the Americans the central and the French the South-western regions. On the German side the war had cost about ten million lives. Thousands of soldiers were prisoners of war.

Fr Kentenich turned sixty on 18 November 1945. After all the trials and sufferings of Dachau it would not have been surprising if he had needed a rest. Humanly speaking that would have been quite understandable. But the opposite happened. He came out of the hell renewed, and believed that he had received confirmation of his conviction that his work bore a divine stamp. He was ready and prepared for new battles. Dachau had made him younger than ever before, he remarked on his arrival in Chile in 1947.

In October 1945 the first "October Week" was organised in Schoenstatt. This is the great annual gathering of the Schoenstatt Family. It served to review the past and to work out the direction for the future. The theme was gratitude. In the following year (1946) attention was focused on the crowning of our Lady. Two crownings were to be renewed and entered into – that which had taken place in 1939 in the shrine, and the crowning of the Mother Thrice Admirable as Queen of the concentration camp. Through this act the Schoenstatt Family professed to our Lady its smallness and its powerlessness in the face of the tremendous tasks she had placed before it; it recognised the great power God had given his Mother, and expressed its readiness to be an instrument in Mary's hand.

Fr Kentenich, who as usual had "his hand on the pulse beat of the times", examined developments in the world, the events and trends in the world, to discover their underlying tendencies and their orientation towards the future. His conclusions were not precisely rosy. With prophetic intuition he realised that Dachau had not been an isolated phenomenon, or an exception. It was a symbol and sign of what could happen on a world-wide scale. From this arose his desire to make others "capable of coping with Dachau", that is, he wanted to help them to acquire the attitude and ability to live in a world that is dominated by totalitarian and atheistic powers; and not merely to survive, but even to develop and conquer.

In the time to come two great fundamental tendencies were to mark his apostolic activity: on the one hand, the development of the Schoenstatt "International" (founded on 18.10.1944 in Dachau), through building a whole network of daughter shrines. ("After my release from the camp it was clear to me that our Lady of Schoenstatt required me to travel the world . . . in order to draw her triumphal chariot through every country and to be a witness to her glory and her masterly education there.") On the other hand, he took the first steps to gain Schoenstatt's official recognition by the hierarchy, both by the German bishops and the Holy See.

His plan to travel the world met with an obstacle: Germany was occupied by the Allies, and the occupation forces allowed no one to travel abroad. On 11 July 1945 Fr Kentenich applied to the French military administration in Coblenz for a pass to go to Switzerland. He only received it three months later. At the same time he had negotiations started in Rome to acquire a diplomatic passport from the Vatican. He managed to get this precious document through an Italian priest, who had been imprisoned with him in Dachau, and who was a personal friend of Monsignor Montini (at that time working in the Secretariate of State and later to become Pope Paul VI).

Early in February 1947 he left for Switzerland, and towards the end of the month went on from there to Rome. Shortly after his arrival he applied for a private audience with Pope Pius XII. He had to wait a long time for an answer, because the Holy Father was very busy. Finally, on 11 March, he was informed by telephone at the Pallottine Generalate, where he was staying, that the audience had been granted for 14 March. It took place towards midday. Fr Kentenich was accompanied by Fr Menningen and by Fr Hoffmann, the Superior General of his community, who introduced him to the Holy Father. He mentioned that Fr Kentenich had just returned from a number of years of imprisonment in the concentration camp at Dachau. The Pope said jokingly, ''But he is looking very well! He must have had a rest-cure there!'' Fr Kentenich presented the purpose of his visit: he had come to Rome to clarify questions about the canonical erection of the Institute of the Sisters of Mary. Since the Apostolic Constitution, ''Provida Mater Ecclesia'', had been published just two days previously, his questions had already been answered. "Is it what you expected? Are you satified with the Constitution?" asked the Pope. Fr Kentenich was very satisfied and thanked the Holy Father most sincerely. He then promised the Holy Father that "he would do all in his power to help to ensure that the 'instituta saecularia' would serve the good of the Church, and in their way help to save the Christian social order". In conclusion he asked for the apostolic blessing for the whole of Schoenstatt, to which the Pope replied, "Oh, gladly, We are very happy to impart our Apostolic Blessing." He then asked, "How are you feeling now? Are you still suffering from the consequences of the concentration camp?" "No, Holy Father, I am in better health than ever before." "Yes," added the Pope smilingly, "you had a rest-cure."

From Rome Fr Kentenich returned to Switzerland, first of all to Fribourg and then to Bern, where he hoped to obtain the visa needed to travel to the countries of South America. Fr August Ziegler, who accompanied him while he carried out the formalities, recalls "I was very doubtful about the whole affair from the beginning, because Fr Kentenich had to have the three visas by midday, since the consulates were closed in the afternoons, and his flight had been booked for the following day". When he reached Bern he first visited the Nunciature and asked for a letter of recommendation in order to facilitate the negotiations for Fr Kentenich's passport. The attempt failed because a secretary discovered some mistake in Fr. Kentenich's papers. So from there Fr Kentenich and Fr Ziegler set out for Kirchenfeld, the suburb where the diplomats had their residences. They encountered many difficulties. Fr Kentenich battled for his visa without a break and without becoming discouraged. "You will see," he told Fr Ziegler, "everything is ready. If Divine Providence has planned that I should leave for South America tomorrow, everything we need will be provided at the right time. You will see, we will have all three visas by midday." And that is what happened. Shortly after midday he did have them – to Fr Ziegler's amazement. "The remarkable way in which everything 'went like clockwork' that morning, the way in which all the difficulties disappeared as though by themselves, showed me that Fr Kentenich was a man of Providence, that is, a man in whose life the hand of Providence showed up with particular clarity."

He touched South American soil for the first time in Brazil. He arrived in Rio de Janeiro on 16.3.1947. At that time the plane did not touch down at the "Galeão" airport, but on an island. The passengers were then brought to the airport by boat. Sr Norberta, at that time the Provincial Superior of the Sisters of Mary in Brazil, was waiting for him. She examined all the little boats with great care as they arrived. Suddenly she saw a white beard. That had to be Fr Kentenich! She watched him disembark – upright and free. She waved, he caught sight of her and waved back. He continued his journey the following day to Porto Alegre where he spent the night with the Marist Brothers. On 18 March he took the train to Santa Maria and arrived as the sun set. He was greeted at the entrance to the house by the sisters who sang songs and made a small speech of welcome. Then he made his way to the chapel and addressed a few words

123

to those present, "I have been led here not merely by natural feelings; I have come to experience our Lady's glories here. . . . I want to discuss with you how we can still further prepare for the glorification of our Lady and spread it further afield."

After a stay of about ten days, he returned to Porto Alegre. From there he visited the various houses of the sisters at Jaraguá do Sul, Rio Negro, Londrina, Jacarezinho, Ribeirão Claro. He was obviously impressed by this first meeting with Schoenstatt in another country and on another continent, ". . . a strange language, strange faces, a foreign nation, and yet the same language, one heart and one soul," he remarked on this occasion. When he was in Londrina on 21.4.1947, he said, "Think of America. They have robbed Europe of the foundation of its culture – Christ. The effect now is that everything is collapsing. Who had been commissioned to give Christ to the world? That is the bearer of Christ. We must show her to the world."

On 9 May 1947 Fr Kentenich flew from Porto Alegre to the "Carrasco" airport, Montevideo. Members of the Schoenstatt Family were there to meet him. They took him by car to Nueva Helvetia (today called Colonia Suiza), a village founded by Swiss immigrants. It is about two hours by car south of Montevideo. The Sisters of Mary had settled there in 1937 and conducted a school for girls. The most characteristic feature of Nueva Helvetia, however, was a little shrine near the school. They had built the first Schoenstatt daughter shrine there during the war. It had been blessed on 18 October 1943. Fr Kentenich was a prisoner in Dachau at the time, but he was fully informed about this completely new undertaking on the part of the sisters at Nueva Helvetia. He discovered in it a prophetic sign. It was as though it was a single mesh of a whole net of daughter shrines that has circled the world until today and is still spreading. Hardly had he arrived than he directed his steps towards the shrine. He was amazed at its similarity to the original shrine in Schoenstatt. "It is remarkably similar," he remarked as he entered.

After he had prayed silently for a few moments, he addressed a few words to the sisters who had gathered there. In the middle of this improvised talk, Fr Amengual, a young, zealous and zestful priest from Spain, who was parish priest of Nueva Helvetia at the time, opened the door carefully, almost shyly. He had been told a great deal about the founder by the sisters, but he was curious to know how he would be received by him. When Fr Kentenich saw him, he interrupted his talk, went up to him, embraced him and addressed him in Latin, "Amicus meus" (my friend). From then on Fr Amengual considered himself in a special way a son of Fr Kentenich.

During his stay in Uruguay, Fr Kentenich gave a talk for the public in the hall of the "Club Católico" in Motevideo. His topic was "The Church's way into the new era". The following morning a summary of this talk appeared in the local newspaper "El dia". According to this report, Fr Kentenich described the present era as a markedly apocalyptic time, that is, a time that is marked by the work of diabolical forces, by brutality and cruelty, and by manipulative fanatacism. He confirmed that the reported atrocities committed during the war and in the concentration camp had really happened. In one and the same country, for example, it is possible to find many criminals and demonic people, and at the same time many heroic and saintly people. The devil had been personally at work behind the atrocities. The world had forgotten that the devil really does exist and work, and that we must always take the presence and the influence of metaphysical evil into account. The ordinary Christian today is aware that there is a battle going on between good and evil, but he forgets that the Evil One cannot be overcome by human forces on their own. The tragedy of modern man consists in this, that he wants to conquer the devil with purely human means. However, this is completely impossible.

On 29 May, accompanied by two Sisters of Mary, he set off by seaplane, the "Sunderlan", from Colonia, Uruguay, for Buenos Aires, and landed at Dock "F" in the Argentinian capital. From there they went by train to Villa Ballester, the first house of the Sisters of Mary in the Argentine (1935). He visited the other houses of the Sisters of Mary and gave talks to German speaking groups, in particular the priests. Fr Santiago Dicks, a missionary of the Holy Family community, recalls the retreat which Fr Kentenich conducted for priests of different religious communities at Villa Calzada: "It took place from 10 to 14 August 1947. I had to travel from Rosario to Villa Calzada, but the long journey was worthwhile. This retreat was a special grace for me. I have never forgotten one thought out of all that Fr Kentenich said: the little events that take place every day are little prophets of God. For me it was a completely new idea that God was speaking to me through these little prophets. Once I had understood this, I felt tremendously enriched. God is speaking to me. . . . I live from this thought still today!''

Mrs Hilde von Malgay belonged to the Catholic Youth of Villa Ballester in 1947. Her first meeting with Fr Kentenich made a deep impression on her. She had recently taken on her first job. She gave half of her first salary to our Lady, placing the money on the altar in the chapel of the German community at Villa Ballester. Someone had told Fr Kentenich about this. ''I was amazed when he commented on it. He never forgot it. When we met later he still remembered the episode, which I thought he must have forgotten long before. On various occasions he said to me, ''Is it true that our Lady repaid your donation with interest?''

With Sr Candida and Sr Ursula to accompany him, Fr Kentenich flew from Buenos Aires to Santiago, Chile, on 23 June. As they flew over the Andes, the plane suddenly entered an airpocket and lost altitude. Once it had regained its normal altitude, Fr Kentenich asked the sisters:

''Well, what did you think now? Did you get a fright? Were you afraid?''

''No, I wasn't afraid. . . It only dropped so suddenly.''

''Why weren't you afraid?''

''We knew that you were with us, Father.''

''You see,'' he replied after a pause, ''the same thing happens in our lives. The heavenly Father is always with us; we have no reason to be afraid.'' When they arrived at the airport, ''Los Cerrillos'', which was at that time on the outskirts of Santiago, they found that the people belonging to the airline had rolled out the red carpet to the gangway of the plane in order to welcome the passenger with a diplomatic passport. That afternoon Fr Kentenich spoke to the members of the Schoenstatt Family who had gathered to meet him. He said, "When I look back and ponder on what the past years have meant according to God's plan, I am reminded of the words of the prophet Jeremiah: 'Go now to those to whom I send you and say whatever I command you. Do not be afraid of them, for I am with you.' This keyword explains why I am here."

He visited the houses belonging to the Sisters of Mary and made contact with the hierarchy, he gave talks and conducted retreats, he was interested in everyone and informed himself about everything. "His journeys," someone testified, "were very pleasant; he made use of the time in the train or car, or wherever he was, he related anecdotes, explained principles, learnt songs and practised them. The table conversations were often greatly extended. Once – he was in Temuco, Chile – the conversation lasted from lunch until into the evening."

On his return journey to Europe he again made a stop in Brazil from the end of August to mid-September. On 7 September, Independence Day, he blessed the foundation stone for the shrine at Santa Maria, in the province Rio Grande do Sul. In view of the start of Brazil's national independence, he dared to draw a comparison between it and the simple ceremony. He asked himself, "Will this ceremony, this event, go down in the history of the Brazilian people as a great day? Why should this not be possible? Since our Lady managed to bring about great things under difficult circumstances in the Old World, why should she not manage to do the same here?" He recalled that there was another Marian shrine in the town, one that was dedicated to the "Mediatrix of all Graces" (Nossa Senhora Medianeira), and he explained the relationship between the two shrines: There our Lady wanted to draw the broad masses of the people to herself, here she wanted to conduct retreats. "She wants to be the great Educator, she wants to be the great Leader." Five days later he flew from Rio de Janeiro to Rome. He reached Schoenstatt on 11 October and with that ended his first world tour. Three days later he conducted the third October Week; its theme was the covenant of love. However his stay in Germany was to be very brief: on 29 December he set out from Geneva – his goal: South Africa. Two days later, on 31 December, he landed punctually at 5 p.m. at the Johannesburg airport. A three months' stay on South African soil had started. During this time he studied the situation in the country, visited the houses of the Sisters of Mary and prepared the way for the spread of Schoenstatt. He came as the messenger of the threefold Schoenstatt message – the message of practical belief in Divine Providence, of the covenant of love with our Lady and of mission-consciousness.

From the first day on Fr Kentenich did not organize his programme according to a fixed schedule, but allowed himself to be directed step by step by Providence, that is, through the people he met, through the needs and wishes of the people who came to him, or through circumstances. He allowed all these to show him what God wanted each time. Before he gave the sisters any orientation or directives, he wanted to get to know the circumstances in the country, the Catholic Church, and above all the people and their problems. During his brief stay he travelled thousands of kilometers, despite the difficulties one can easily imagine. A sister recalled, "We sometimes had to book a seat in the train at almost no notice, or we had to find someone who was prepared to drive long distances. This was because new doors repeatedly opened up and our father wanted to go through them each time." If someone had reservations about difficulties that might possibly arise, he answered calmly, "Our Lady will see to it. If our faith in Divine Providence is strong enough, she is able to do more than we dare to hope for. So you must always have more daring, more certainty of victory."

In Germany it seems to have been generally held that Fr Kentenich would have plenty of spare time in South Africa. But, as he wrote in a letter, "there was so much to do that the day with all its hours was not long enough. The night had, as usual, to come to my aid." A Sister of Mary testified, "Fr Kentenich worked almost day and night. However, he always appeared calm. He was open for the many demands made on him, but he consistently avoided wasting any time."

Bishop Hennemann of Cape Town appreciated Fr Kentenich highly and felt like a protector towards him. Out of concern for Fr Kentenich's health, since he seldom or never rested, he sent his secretary to him one day. This priest was to take him out for a few hours on a sightseeing tour. "If the bishop wants it," said Fr Kentenich, "I have to accept the offer". He asked two Sisters of Mary to accompany him as interpreters. As they got into the car he said with a smile to the driver, "I am always ready for sacrifice". Once they had reached a point where there was a particularly beautiful view, the car stopped and the driver began to explain what they saw spread out below them – the sea, the city, the mountains. Fr Kentenich stood for a few moments and took in the beauty. Then he said, "Majestas Domini – the majesty of God! All is light, air and water!" Turning to the sisters he continued, "Come, let us get in. I have come to proclaim the covenant of love." And on the way home they had to explain it to the bishop's secretary.

Wherever he stayed, he was followed by mountains of post from all over the world. The postman at Cathcart was amazed at the quantities of letters he had to deliver, and remarked that a very important person must have been staying there. Fr Kentenich read every letter he received. He could recognise the writer from the writing and was able to recall the letters written by that person in the past, even when he did not have them to hand. He was obviously unable to answer them all. However, the most important ones, or those from people who were in difficult circumstances, were answered immediately. He made use of every free moment of the day to see to his post. "I was impressed," one of his secretaries related, "by the reverence with which he treated every letter. Before placing a letter in the waste paper basket, he first blessed the writer. You could see that every person, even the least important, was very important to him, and how he lived with every one of his followers. . . ."

Fr Kentenich showed great respect for the black people of the country. Once, when he met a beggar in the street, he raised his hat and bowed to him slightly. "I shall never forget," one sister reported, "how Fr Kentenich adapted himself to the thinking of the ordinary people when he

spoke to them about our Lady and the covenant of love".
Early in April 1948 he left South Africa for Brazil, where
the blessing of the first daughter shrine on Brazilian soil
took place on 11 of that month. On 25 he blessed
the foundation stone for the shrine at Londrina in the
state of Paraná. He was soon to go to the United States.
At the end of May, in mid-winter, he crossed the Andes.
"On 25 May the plane crossed the Andes on the way to
Chile," he wrote in his travel chronicle. "The journey
was very dangerous. We spent an hour circling Santiago,
but could not land because of the fog; then we flew on
to Antofagasta, a journey of three-and-a-half hours.
From there we finally reached our destination in the
night from 26 to 27. I wanted to fly to North America
on Monday, but I could not get a seat. . . Tomorrow,
on 4 June, the 'Panagra' will take me to North America,
first of all to Chicago. We landed on schedule on 5
June." Fr Kentenich visited the USA for the first time
from 5 June to 6 September. This visit had the character
of a study tour, the aim of which was to get to know the
soul of that country which sets the tone for the West and
which is the chief world power. The people he met and
the impressions he gained during this stay enabled him
to find points of contact between the American character
and Schoenstatt. He undertook this journey for the sake
of his own home country, because the United States
exercised a great influence on Europe, and in particular
Germany, through its political policies. He considered
it of fundamental importance for someone who wanted
to lead his people in an enlightened manner "to get to
know the East and the West with their open and secret
intentions and spiritual currents". Through his contact

with Slavic prisoners in Dachau he had had an opportunity to get to know the character and the spirituality of the peoples of Eastern Europe. He was now being offered an opportunity to take in the Western soul in the same way. He wrote down the results of his obvservations in the so-called "American Report". This report is more than a diary of his journey, and aims at being a "handbook of the history of the times and education". Fr Kentenich was well aware of the difficulties and risks of his undertaking (it should be kept in mind that this was 1948. The USA had just won the war and Germany was a conquered nation. Besides this, thirty years ago the North American people had quite a different outlook on life to that of today.) Fr Kentenich knew that he was the main bearer of a movement that had a clear mission for the world. This tendency to be world-wide was innate to him and had always been at work in him. Ever since the foundation of the "International" in Dachau, it had become a conscious and clearly defined goal that no longer left him any peace. The words of St Peter in answer to our Lord, "At your word I shall pay out the net," exactly expressed what Fr Kentenich felt during this journey, and what moved him: "It accompanied me on my journey to and through North America, and it gave content, direction, form and security to every event and experience."

True to his method – of observing life, making comparisons, tracing everything back to ultimate principles and seeking practical applications – he dwelt on certain problems at greater length; he reflected on the racial problems, the question of vocations to the priesthood and of adaptation to the country. He sketched the

"American character" in a very original way, and showed the problem it posed. Even Americans found his description novel, it "had the effect of a revelation". Fr Kentenich came across an expression that attempted to describe the typical character of North America as being a "melting pot". That is to say, this huge country melts, dissolves, indeed destroys every original national feature of its immigrants as though in a melting pot, so that everything that is independent or original has to disappear. In its place appears something new, the so-called "American character". No one, however, was in a position to say just what this was. Fr Kentenich did not like the idea of a melting pot. He replaced it with the symbol of a bell. "America's character, as God wants it and as it will serve the people, may be looked upon as a bell, which is cast from many valuable metals, but which is not yet complete and so does not give out a full note. If its sound is to be pure, every metal added to it must remain true to itself, this must be promoted with great care and each must combine itself with the valuable qualities of the other peoples. The structure that will ultimately result will be the original soul of the American people, which is not an addition and multiplication of individual, natural qualities, but should be seen as something new."

Fr Kentenich also encountered the following fact: a large number of Germans made a radical break with their origins in order to adapt themselves to North American ways. This was not a sound development. He objected to it and insisted: "It is quite possible to become all things to all men without losing or denying yourself and your national character."

During his three months' stay, he visited Chicago, New York, Washington, Omaha (Nebraska) and Miami. On 6 September he flew back to South America. On 18 October he blessed the foundation stone for the future shrine for Bellavista, on the outskirts of Santiago de Chile, at the foot of the Andes.

Fr Kentenich spent the rest of this year and the whole of 1949 in South America. He spent his time in Chile, the Argentine, Uruguay and Brazil. He only returned to Europe in 1950, in order to take part in Vincent Pallotti's beatification on 22.1 in Rome. His volume of work, the constant change from one place to another, and the adaptation to other climatic conditions this necessitated, the strain of the journeys, all far exceeded, humanly speaking, the strength of a sixty-three-year-old man. However, it seemed as though nothing could affect Fr Kentenich. "Body and soul are completely able to cope with the strains of the journey and the rapid and fully laden rhythm of work," he wrote to the Archbishop of Treves. "Just as in Dachau, so here my powers seem to multiply in the face of battle and danger, overwork and deprivation" (27.5.1948).

On his return from Dachau he had made a second strategic decision: he wanted to do all in his power to have Schoenstatt recognised and sanctioned by the Church. "We don't want to exist next to the Church," he explained at the 1945 October Week, "nor do we want to be over the Church, but in the Church... That is the reason for the strong urge to integrate our realm into the hierarchy, that is the reason for our dependence each time on the parish and the diocese." Such a process requires time. As the centuries of the Church's history have taught

135

us, this usually does not happen without tensions and problems. Schoenstatt was to be no exception to this rule. A first, positive step towards this goal was the canonical erection of the Institute of the Sisters of Mary, which Fr Kentenich had founded in 1926. On 20 May 1948 Archbishop Bornewasser of Treves undertook this act of official recognition of the new type of person and community which Fr Kentenich had been trying to educate since 1912 – 1914. Almost simultaneously difficulties began to arise in Germany. Critical voices were raised against Schoenstatt, and particularly against Fr Kentenich himself. There were bishops who did not agree to the spread of the Movement in their dioceses, because they feared that conflicts with existing organizations might arise. However, the core of the difficulties was to be found elsewhere: in specific elements of Schoenstatt's spirituality (the so-called ''special ideas''). The Auxiliary Bishop of Bamberg, Bishop Arthur Michael Landgraf, had prepared an assessment of Schoenstatt for the Autumn Conference of the German Bishops in 1948. The bishops had to react. The first step was then taken. The diocese of Treves, to which Schoenstatt belongs, decided to conduct a Visitation in Schoenstatt to clarify the situation, and this took place from 19 – 28 February. The result was basically positive and well-disposed. However, the Visitator made a few remarks about the eductional system of the Sisters of Mary, and the hymns and prayers of the Movement. These, and only these, should be revised. On 27 April the Archbishop of Treves sent Fr Kentenich (who was in South America) the Visitator's report and asked for his comment. Fr Kentenich decided to answer in the form

136

of an objective, scientific treatise, which was dated 31 May 1949 and was directed to the Bishop of Treves in the hope that it would reach many bishops from there. What was the core of the problem?

The Visitator's criticism concerned Fr Kentenich's rôle in the Schoenstatt Family, and in particular in the family of the Sisters of Mary. (It was feared that he exercised an exaggerated influence on persons, and that personal attachment to him in Schoenstatt could become more important one day than attachment to our Lady and the shrine.) Fr Kentenich believed that these remarks revealed a certain mentality, a way of seeing and living reality, which led to a separation between truth and life, between theory and practice, between what is human and divine. The mental attitude just described promotes a process of disintegration which prevents Christianity from unfolding its full vitality and creativity in the face of collectivism (which Fr Kentenich considered to be advancing powerfully and radically destroying our organically grown culture). He called this mentality ''mechanistic thinking'', and he saw in it the ''bacillus which is shaking the present-day Western world to its deepest depths''; a sickness under which he himself had suffered in his youth, and which he had been able to overcome thanks to his total self-surrender to our Lady, who always gives us an organic way of thinking. ''Mechanistic thinking'' gives rise to a crisis that is particularly noticeable in two important points: in our Lady herself (the relationship of the human being to the divine order) and in the figure of the father (relationship to the human order). Basically this mentality cannot grasp correctly what the rôle of created beings is as the expression

137

of, the way to and the protection for our relationship to the Creator (both our Lady and the father are human creatures, even though Mary alone has been conceived without original sin, and is therefore the most exalted of all mere creatures). Fr Kentenich received the letter from the Archbishop of Treves while he was in the Argentine. He had planned to travel from there to Uruguay, and then on to Chile, where he blessed the shrine at Bellavista on 20 May 1949 after a cloudburst. On 31 May, before he sent off the first part of his answer to Treves (the completed work consisted of a number of parts, which were sent off one after the other, and together filled over three hundred pages), he placed what he had written on the altar of the shrine at Bellavista. ''We have gathered here in this quiet evening hour to present our Lady solemnly with the common work we have completed for her.'' In this memorable address, which has gone down in Schoenstatt's history as its third milestone, Fr Kentenich spoke with prophetic force about the powerful advance of collectivism. He saw that the Western world was threatened by an earth-shattering danger. According to his interpretation, the Mother of God has a great task to fulfil for the future of the West. Put briefly: ''We are concerned here with uncovering and healing the root, the ultimate germ, of the illness under which the soul of the Werstern world is suffering – mechanistic thinking.''

At the same time he was well aware that his treatise would wound noble hearts in Germany very deeply, that the ideas he was putting forward would give rise to bitter indignation and call forth hard counter-attacks. He took into account that it would not be surprising if a powerful, common front of influential men was to form in opposition to him and his work. Humanly speaking it was not impossible that the whole undertaking (to help to renew the Church by sincere and constructive criticism) could fail. Nevertheless he felt obliged to take the risk: "Whoever has a mission must fulfil it, even if the way leads through the darkest and deepest abyss, even when deathleap after deathleap is required! A prophet's mission always includes a prophet's fate."

This is what happened. Fr Kentenich's answer awakened a powerful wave of opposition to him and to Schoenstatt (since the two cannot be separated). In July 1949 Fr Kentenich received a letter from the diocesan Chancery at Treves: On behalf of the German Bishops' Conference, a number of expressions that were current in Schoenstatt were forbidden. In April 1950 the diocesan Visitator presented his reservations about Fr Kentenich's pedagogy to Rome.

In November of that year he requested the Holy See to conduct an Apostolic Visitation of Schoenstatt, and in particular of the Sisters of Mary. This task was entrusted to Fr Sebastian Tromp SJ, Professor at the Gregoriana and Consultor to the Holy Office. He met Fr Kentenich for the first time at the beginning of May 1951, when the latter arrived back from South America. He placed the following alternative before him: Either to separate himself from his work of his own accord (it might then be possible for him to return to it soon afterwards); or to be separated from it by an authoritative decree, in which case he could count upon never returning from exile. Once again Fr Kentenich found himself faced with a momentous decision. What should he do? What was

139

God's will? At the time he was accompanied by Fr Menningen, his faithful disciple and co-worker; Fr Kentenich asked him to share in the decision that had to be made. He sent the following answer to Fr Tromp via Fr Adalbert Turowski, his Superior General: Out of faithfulness to his work he would not consider separating himself from it of his own accord; should, however, the Church authorities command it, he would obey immediately. Events pressed hard upon each other. On 31 July he was dismissed from his office as Director General of the Sisters of Mary by a decree of the Apostolic Visitator. Another decree (of 30 September) laid down that he might no longer reside in Schoenstatt itself. A third decree (of 1 December) ordered him to leave Europe. Since he had already accepted certain engagements he was allowed to carry them out. He therefore conducted an Educational Congress (2 – 5 October), and the October Week (15 – 19 October). His closing words at the educational course are a good reflection of his attitude of soul at that time, and his vision of the future: "All who have received a Marian mission must be prepared for constant battle. They share in our Lord's fate. The less prospect there is of victory, and the more we confront Goliath like David, the more we will remain true to our Lady and say: If people rob me of my good name, I shall care for your honour. The more we try to care for her in every circumstance, the more certain you may be: She will set up an unexampled monument to herself and the Triune God in our community, a monument to her power, her kindness, her wisdom." On 22 October 1951 he left Schoenstatt on his way into exile.

11. THE LONG WAY OF THE CROSS

The first stop Fr Kentenich made en route into exile (he would only return to Schoenstatt fourteen years later) was at the Premonstratensian Monastery, Berg Sion, near Uznach in Switzerland, where he had conducted retreats before and after the Second World War. In the course of the weeks he spent there, he wrote a study "Key to an understanding of Schoenstatt" by hand. This work was written for Fr A Bea (at that time consultor to the Holy Office, later Cardinal and head of the Secretariate for Christian Unity), and was designed to offer a very concise yet overall insight into Schoenstatt according to its "leading ideas and motivating forces". Four weeks later on 23 November, he travelled to Rome. Early in 1952 he paid a brief visit to Valle di Pompeii and Naples, in order to get to know the Marian shrine that had so decisively inspired Schoenstatt's foundation. "I was away for two days," he wrote on 5 January 1952 to Fr Josef Fischer, "in Naples and Pompeii. I visited Bartolo Longo's grave there and I entered more deeply into his work and his world of ideas." He was again impressed by the similarity between Schoenstatt and Bartolo Longo's foundation: faith in the supernatural character of the work and the opposition it constantly aroused. The decree banishing Fr Kentenich from Europe had been published on 1 December 1951. Since, however, he still had not received a residence permit for the USA, where he was meant to live, he was permitted to go to South America until he had received the necessary papers. That was why, despite seemingly insurmountable obstacles, he was able to attend the blessing of the shrine at Nuevo Schoenstatt in the Argentine. The blessing had been arranged for Sunday, 20 January. This was the tenth anniversary of the day he had freely decided to go to the concentration camp. He arrived on Thursday, 17 January, in an SAS plane, landing at Ezeiza where he was met by a handful of people, who immediately took him to Nuevo Schoenstatt. Three days later he blessed the shrine, the first in the Argentine. His presence was a great joy for the sisters, but also a great suffering. They knew joy because, despite all the difficulties, he had been able to come for the blessing. They knew suffering because a decree of the Holy Office prevented them from speaking to him. The blessing of the shrine took place in the morning during the celebration of the Eucharist. Fr Kentenich stood as erect as ever, but it was painful for him to experience how the sisters were suffering. (He had told Fr Menningen at the Zürich station that what affected him personally did not matter to him, but what was done to the sisters pierced him to the heart.)

His sermon, in which he depicted the mission of the shrine as a sign of faith, unity, battle and victory, ended with the significant words, "We shall be victorious because we are dying. We will be victorious because we have consecrated ourselves to our Lady, and because, in keeping with God's plans, she has foreseen much suffering for us, and because we are prepared to surrender everything: our own honour, our own lives, our home, everything we have been allowed to bring about. We shall be victorious because we are dying."

That afternoon the first pilgrimage came to the newly

blessed shrine. The parish priest of Florencio Varela and a notable member of the faithful took part. In his address, Fr Kentenich made a few statements that have since proved to be prophetic. "We are approaching a time," he said, "that will be so Marian in character that its like will not have been seen in the world". And with reference to this first group of pilgrims standing around the shrine, he added, "Behind us we see the thousands and millions who will come here after us". From 14 February to 19 March, at the height of summer, he conducted a Tertianship for the Pallottine Fathers in Santa Maria, Brazil. In this period he gave 73 talks: 63 for the Fathers, nine for the Schoenstatt Family and one for the Marist Brothers. In Santa Maria the same painful situation was repeated that had taken place in the Argentine as a result of the decree forbidding him to speak to the Sisters of Mary. Imagine what it must be like if the father of a family comes home and because of a Church ban is not allowed to speak to his sons and daughters. Fr Kentenich's words of greeting referred to these circumstances. "My dear Schoenstatt Family, this time it is difficult for me and it is also difficult for you. It is difficult for me to address a word of greeting to you. And it is difficult for you to understand and interpret correctly the words that I am speaking to you. (...) The masterstroke will consist in this, that outwardly I have to be reserved towards the sisters. . . God wants it this way – and so: I always do what pleases the Father. Inwardly everything remains unchanged."

In Bellavista, Chile, his last stop before leaving for Milwaukee, USA, he told the assembled Schoenstatt Family, "Our task as instruments consists in carefully considering God's plans, and in giving ourselves to him without reserve, even when our path leads into darkness, and even when it descends into the abyss; not only 'even when', but very particularly when it does so''.

In May he wrote Monsignor Joseph Schmitz in Germany an important letter in which he raised fundamental issues in explanation of the storm that had broken out over Schoenstatt and particularly over himself. He underlined: ''... because we have the future of the world and Church so strongly and constantly in view − without on that account losing connection in theory or in practice with the past and present − it is easily understandable that we should come into collision with those Church circles which are one-sidedly orientated to the past, which only, or almost exclusively, cling to the past, and which are unable to take the new image of the world, society, the Church and mankind into their field of vision and interests''. This was the reason for the constant tensions in which Schoenstatt had grown up, and which may not merely be regarded as something negative, but which has on the contrary proved to be a creative principle. To those who regarded his analysis of the times and the world situation as correct, but who objected to his open criticism and his frankness in dealing with Church authorities, he answered: Seen from a purely human point of view, he should rather have chosen a different course of action. But he believed that God had shown him this way and no other. ''When God speaks,'' he wrote, ''when he speaks clearly, when he speaks challengingly, the creature has to be silent. .. Then no excuses count, no plea that one has a heavy tongue, or that there will be bad consequences for oneself and others.

144

'Ibis nobis!' You have to go! You must go! That is the authoritative word of the Lord – and with that every objection is cut short. So I went. I would do exactly the same thing a second, a third, a fourth time, even if the consequences were still more painful.''

Fr Kentenich's departure had been fixed for the beginning of June. On 6 June Fr Carlos Sehr, at that time the Pallottine Provincial Superior in Chile and a faithful collaborator of Fr Kentenich, returned to Bellavista in great annoyance. He had just fetched the new black suit Fr Kentenich had had made for his stay in the USA, and in the city centre someone had stolen it out of his car. As a result Fr Kentenich had to postpone his departure until a new suit had been made. In the end he left for the United States on 20 June from ''Los Cerrillos'' airport. As he said goodbye he remarked, ''… this time I find it hard to leave, because the bond uniting us has become so deep and warm''.

On the following day he landed at Milwaukee airport. This is a growing city on the shores of Lake Michigan, about two hours away from Chicago. Three large national groups – North Americans, Germans and Poles – have brought about the dynamic development of the city. It is well known for its engineering works (Allis Chalmers), its breweries (Schlitz), and for Marquette University, which is run by the Jesuits. The Pallottine Society had set up a Provincial House there. The Provincial Superior at the time was Fr Haas. Fr Kentenich had turned sixty-six. His hair and beard were almost completely white. But the new arrival was not a used up and exhausted man. He had a firm tread, upright bearing and exuded firmness and inner freedom. ''Whoever has

God as his staff and support is always calm and relaxed. I went with this staff through the prison and concentration camp, and am now as calm as I was then. We need only have one passion: to belong to God, to serve God, to complete his works."

His new home was situated in the western part of Milwaukee in the Holy Cross Parish, 5424 Blue Mound Road. Opposite the presbytery there was the Calvary Cemetery laid out as a large park. In spring it was decked in green and in winter it was covered with a heavy blanket of snow. A few broad paths and a number of narrower paths led to the graves. Here and there friendly squirrels hopped over the paths or clambered up the trees. For thirteen years Fr Kentenich took a walk almost daily in the cemetery. Sometimes he was alone, usually, however, he was accompanied by a visitor. To one side of the church was the usual parish school, which is typical of every parish in the USA. On the other side, facing Wisconsin Avenue, there was a large lawn that was always well cared for and hence always green. In 1954, that is, two years after Fr Kentenich's arrival, a shrine of the Mother Thrice Admirable was built behind the community's house. From then on, in summer as in winter, Fr Kentenich celebrated Holy Mass there punctually at 5.50 a.m. In order to make good use of the spare time he now had at his disposal, he began to write. In this way "Chronicle Notes", "Commentaries" and other studies ensued, that is, treatises and comments on definite events.

Early in 1954 one of his confrères asked him for a cycle of sermons on our Lady for Lent. That was the origin of the "Lenten Sermons" which grew to become a book (published, so far only in German, under the title "Mary, Mother and Educator, an applied Mariology", 1973). This was quite typical of him – wherever he could, he bore witness to our Lady's mission. These sermons of 1954 have to be seen in the framework of the Marian Year as a gift to the Mother of God. Early in 1959 a student at Marquette University had to prepare a scientific study on Schoenstatt's educational system and was searching for literature on the subject. In order to help her, Fr Kentenich wrote a study entitled: "What is my philosophy of education?" In it he stated that one of the causes of social unrest in our time is the crisis of the father, the problem of the father. "The tragedy of the new era is basically the tragedy of the father. Therefore, one of the most central tasks of education as a whole is to care for the re-birth of the father."

In another work ("On the relationship in tension between office and charism") from the year 1957, he took up a theme that was to play a very important part in the text of the Second Vatican Council (cf Lumen Gentium 12) some years later: the charisms in the Church and their relationship to the hierarchy. His discussion of the figure of the prophet is of particular interest: "The prophet appears in opposition to the existing order; that is the actual reason for his appearance. ... Of course, this 'departure', no matter how it has taken place and takes place, includes an ambivalence that cannot be overlooked – it can renew the Church, but it can also cause a split in the Church. The prophet becomes a heretic when he absolutises his position, when he separates himself from the community of the Church. Therefore every heretic is at bottom a prophet who has failed ... If the opposition does not turn into conflict, it becomes fruitful, it is accepted into the Church. Obviously, this cannot happen immediately.''

During the long years in exile, Fr Kentenich was able to lead a very ordered and constant rhythm through the day, one that was quite different to the years of intense activity in the past and his international journeys (1947 – 1951). He rose very early because he celebrated Holy Mass at 5.50 a.m. He spent the mornings answering his post, dictating to his secretary or receiving visitors. (He adapted rapidly to circumstances, or, we would do better to say, to what God wanted of him through them each time.) He had lunch, but not supper, with the other priests belonging to his community. Fr Benjamin Pereira, at present Rector of the Seminary of the Archdiocese of Santiago, Chile, spent some months in the same house with him. He describes Fr Kentenich's fraternal, social attitude: ''At table he was always concerned about the others. He adapted himself to the topic of conversation raised by the others and joined in, even if the topic was of no special importance. Everything was important to him. In all probability he knew the other occupants of the house better than anyone else, although many appeared indifferent towards him. He was a pleasant confrère in the community, simple and unassuming.''

He celebrated our Lady's feasts in a special way. He always said, ''Mary's feasts are days of grace''. (In May, Mary's month, he suggested that each May day should be held as a day belonging to Mary, and in this way transformed into a day of grace.) On such days of festival he used to devote half an hour to reading about Mary.

His secretary read him something about Mary; he listened, then he began his day's work. Humanly speaking his situation was one of impenetrable darkness. There seemed no way out. Fr Kentenich trusted blindly that in the end Mary would be victorious and so reveal her power, kindness and faithfulness once more. "Mary will glorify herself," he used to say. "We may not become tired and discouraged, but do our share. But our Lady has reserved my liberation and that of the Schoenstatt Family to herself." In 1958, when he turned 73, he thanked a small, inner circle for their good wishes and spoke about his Marian mission. Taking the Apostle Paul's mission to proclaim the mystery of Christ to the world as his starting point, he explained how he saw himself. "It was and is my mission to proclaim our Lady, to unveil her to our times, with the specific mission she has to carry out from her Schoenstatt shrines for our present era."

From time to time he took an outing to Lake Michigan with friends. They usually planned the outing in such a way that they reached the shores of the lake when no one else was around. Fr Kentenich liked going there. Maria Kleinmeyer, his secretary, recalls: Fr Kentenich enjoyed our happiness just like a true father. He used to throw pebbles into the water, and drew our attention to the concentric circles that formed, rather like a small whirlpool. He often used this image in his sermons. He explained that the Mother of God can be compared to a whirlpool which draws us with irresistable force towards Christ. When he was speaking about our Lady's dignity, nobility and power, he liked to compare her with a vast ocean, the one shore of which we can see, but the other shore lies outside our range of vision. This is something like the way it is with Mary, whose dignity, nobility and power are endless, as it were. He knew how to arrange his time so that he always had time for all who came to him. Each one felt personally accepted and taken in. At Christmas 1958, a Chilian agricultural engineer, Victor Alamos, spent a week as a guest in the Holy Cross Parish. He was able to have a discussion with Fr Kentenich almost every day, and they covered the most varied topics. On one occasion, as he entered Fr Kentenich's room, he saw a plate of grapes standing on his desk. Fr Kentenich laughed and said, "Victor, I knew you were coming so I went to the kitchen and stole these grapes for you". On another occasion he had been speaking about engagement, married life and sexuality. As he said good bye to his young visitor, who was obviously satisfied with the answers, he said, "And now my wish for you is that you may dream of your girl-friend today".

Fr Kentenich received an enormous number of letters from all over the world every day, and he tried to keep abreast with each day's arrivals. He read every letter, he answered them when a serious problem had been raised or if someone had expressed a definite wish. He often received telephone calls from people in Milwaukee, because he was their confessor and spiritual director, but calls also came from other parts of the country and from overseas. His telephone rang during the day, and more than once during the night. In 1959 he was appointed pastor to the German community in Milwaukee. From then on he celebrated Holy Mass at 10 a.m. on Sundays in the lower church of St Michael's. Someone usually drove him there. At 9.40 a.m. he walked downstairs to the lower church. In order to pay honour to the fact that it was Sunday, he wore a black hat (in summer a Panama hat). In the sacristy he vested silently, went with his hand over his hair and beard before a small mirror in order to ensure that everything was in place, and waited until the pendulum clock had struck ten. Then he walked to the altar.

He celebrated Holy Mass recollectedly and with great simplicity. His sermon was long – usually half an hour – but no one noticed the time. "You thought only ten minutes had passed," one of his congregation recalls. A member of the choir had this to say about his sermons: "His sermons were often too high for me. But one day I shall tell my children of the old priest with the white beard who Sunday after Sunday preached about God with such certainty and enthusiasm that you thought he had met God personally and was just coming from him to tell us what he had experienced." After Holy Mass he always spent a few minutes in thanksgiving before the altar. Once someone wanted to speak to him urgently. He was told, "Father, someone wants to speak to you urgently, but you haven't yet said your thanksgiving". He replied, "We sometimes have to leave God in order to serve others," and went towards the person concerned. He heard confessions in St Michael's church at 4 p.m. on Saturdays. A considerable number of the faithful came to his confessional in the hope of receiving counsel and forgiveness.

Once a year Fr Kentenich celebrated a Holy Mass for the Apatines, a group of Hungarian refugees who gathered to celebrate one of their feasts. In 1965 this Mass took place in the open. The improvised altar had been placed close to a highway, and the noise of the cars and lorries could easily be heard. In his sermon Fr Kentenich said that although not all of them were holy, yet it was their merit that they had preserved the substance of their faith. In conclusion he wished them much joy in their celebration. ''Don't drink too much,'' he called out laughingly, ''and play the music of the good old days so that the older members can join in the dancing''. His pastoral work for the German community had two focal points: to strengthen the faith and to promote community life. In order to achieve this aim he initiated a number of things: he encouraged the formation of a choir in order to make Holy Mass more beautiful and dignified; he issued a journal, the ''Heimatklänge'' (Sounds from Home), to which he also contributed articles; he organized a monthly pilgrimage to the shrines of our Lady of Schoenstatt in Milwaukee (1954), Philip Neri and, then years later, to Waukesha. On Monday evenings he gave public talks for married people about marriage and family life in the light of the Gospel and the mystery of Mary.

And so the years in Milwaukee passed. Meanwhile, in Europe, particularly in Germany, a bitter battle had broken out over him and his foundation. On the one hand there were difficulties with the German Episcopate, which had asked Rome for the Apostolic Visitation that was conducted from 1951 – 1953. Well informed sources heard that a completed decree for the dissolution of all Schoenstatt Communities had reached Pope Pius XII's desk. However, it did not receive the Pope's signature. On the contrary, in 1953 Pope Pius XII suddenly and unexpectedly declared that the Visitation had ended. At the same time a conflict had broken out between Schoenstatt and the Pallottine Society, to which Fr Kentenich belonged. At bottom two contradictory concepts of Schoenstatt had come into collision. The Pallottines considered Schoenstatt as no more than a continuation of Pallotti's foundation. That is to say, there was only one pole for the whole work: Vincent Pallotti. Schoenstatt (that is, Fr Kentenich) saw things differently. There was not just the one pole, there were two – this is the "bipolar" concept. Schoenstatt was a new foundation; Fr Kentenich had called it into existence in the event of 18 October 1914, and Pallotti had had no influence on this day. These two concepts, as one can easily understand, gave rise to various consequences. Those who upheld the "unipolar concept" maintained that Schoenstatt was dependent on the Pallottines, it was their external work. According to the "bipolar concept", Schoenstatt is essentially a federal structure in which the Secular Institutes belonging to it are independent entities separate from each other. The Pallottines, as the main "supporting and moving part", were simply "primus inter pares", the first among equals. Fr Kentenich considered this federal structure essential for Schoenstatt's incorporation into the Church; the Apostolic League, and the Peoples' and Pilgrims' Movement, should work on the diocesan level in dependence on the local Ordinary.

This controversy dragged on for more than a decade. The battle was waged on two fronts: the "diplomatic" and the "heroic" fronts, as Fr Kentenich described them. The first front referred to human action, to struggling to bring the truth to light, to the legitimate battle for

153

a just judgement based on facts. The other front, which Fr Kentenich considered to be of decisive importance, was designed to draw down God's grace through prayer and sacrifice, and to intercede for God's intervention in events. While the founder spent long years in exile in Milwaukee, a powerful trend of prayer and sacrifice came into existence in the Schoenstatt Family. Once again they experienced the interwovenness of destinies between the father and founder and his family, in much the same way as in the concentration camp years. Just as at that time, Fr Kentenich's return was to be a common work: the victory of solidarity lived to its final consequences. In these years many members of the Schoenstatt Family offered their lives as a ransom for the founder's release. In more than one instance God obviously accepted the offer.

In November 1962, Cardinal Joseph Frings, Chairman of the German Bishops' Conference, with the support of Cardinals Julius Döpfner, Raúl Silva Henriquez and Laureanus Rugambwa, presented a petition to Pope John XXIII, asking him to transfer Schoenstatt's case from the jurisdiction of the Holy Office to that of the Congregation for Religious, which should then work out a new General Statute for the Movement. In January 1963 Pope John XXIII gave the green light for working out this proposal. The following July he died. His successor, Pope Paul VI confirmed the decision of his predecessor. On 3 December 1963 the Congregation for Religious appointed Bishop Joseph Höffner (at that time Bishop of Münster) the ''custos et moderator'' of Schoenstatt as a whole, with Monsignor Wilhelm Wissing (at that time director of the Catholic Offices in Bonn) as his assistant. At the same time Fr Hilario Albers, the then Provincial

Superior of the Dominicans in Ecuador, was commissioned to carry out a new Visitation of Schoenstatt, both in Germany and the other centres throughout the world. The unanimous decision of the German Bishops' Conference (at the Session from 17 – 19 February at Hofheim/Taunus) in favour of Schoenstatt's independence was a decisive event. When the Schoenstatt Family had gathered for the 1964 October Week, which was at the same time the celebration of the Golden Jubilee of its foundation (18.10.1914 – 1964), the decree of the Holy See was announced (drawn up on 6.10.1964 and published on 12.10). It decreed Schoenstatt's independence. At the same time, a new General Statute, which had been drawn up by Fr Albers, came into force, and Monsignor Wilhelm Wissing was appointed Apostolic Administrator of Schoenstatt. The new administrator was faced with the difficult task of completing the separation of Schoenstatt from the Pallottines, of working out a new and final General Statute, and of providing a new "supporting and moving priests' community" for Schoenstatt.

The final problem remained, without doubt the most difficult one – Fr Kentenich's reinstatement. In July 1965 Fr Menningen was surprised to receive an invitation to an audience with Cardinal Ottaviani, at that time the Prefect of the Holy Office. This audience took place on 6 July. It was agreed that Fr Kentenich would be summoned to Rome in October, in order that through direct contact some solution to the problem could be found. Meanwhile Monsignor Wissing went to Milwaukee to get into personal contact with Fr Kentenich, and a member of the Holy Office did the same in writing. Fr Kentenich

Seven Sorrows, he celebrated Holy Mass as usual in the shrine at 5.50 a.m. Towards 7 p.m. all his friends from Milwaukee and the surrounding districts had gathered for a ceremony of leave-taking in the shrine. Fr Kentenich began to speak, "Now, I have no idea which form of address I may use. Should I say: My dear German compatriots? Yes, I have also to take leave of them. In a certain sense we are all compatriots. Compatriots, that is to say, we are all longing for the same land." He then tried to summarise the results of his experiences in those years in Milwaukee. He expressed them briefly in three wishes, which he formulated as follows: "Child, do not forget your Mother! Child, do not forget the mercies of God, the Eternal Father! Child, do not forget your misery!" In conclusion he said that he hoped to see everyone soon again. If God restored his freedom, he would soon be there again. But he would only be able to return for a time, because he had many obligations, to say thank you "to all Schoenstatt members, yes, all without exception, who have stood so faithfully by the flag in all the years and in all the other countries".

On the following day, 16 September, he celebrated Holy Mass as usual in the shrine. He wore a red vestment, because it was the feast of the martyrs Cornelius and Cyprian. The service took somewhat longer than usual because so many received Holy Communion. At 8 a.m. he returned to the shrine again to say goodbye. (It was the last time he was to enter it.) As he went in someone presented him with a bunch of red roses. He knelt in the middle pew on the right and said a short prayer. After a hymn had been sung, he went forward and gave the blessing. He was then taken to the General Mitchell Airport accompanied by a procession of cars. They arrived at 8.35 a.m. He was due to enter the plane half an hour later. The people at the airport were surprised by the crowd that stormed into the departure lounge and encircled an elderly priest with a white beard, whom they photographed constantly. "The officials of the Northwest Airlines were more than somewhat amazed," Fr Alessandri reports, "when this regiment of Sisters of Mary refused to halt at the barrier. Before the eyes of the controlling officials they simply pushed forward with us to the foot of the plane's gangway. Fr Kentenich climbed the steps slowly and waved. Two fingers of his upraised hand made a V, the sign of victory. The Schoenstatt Family stood below and sang. We all felt that it was a moment of joy and of pain at the same time. Many of us had tears in our eyes." After about two hours' flight the plane landed at John F Kennedy Airport, New York. There he was awaited by two friends, who were priests, and about forty Puerto Ricans, all of them simple labourers. "As Fr Kentenich approached," Fr Alessandri relates, "they began to sing 'Schoenstatt, my great love' with great enthusiasm, and as he joined them they called out 'Viva la Mater' – 'long live our Lady' – and 'Viva el Padre Fundador' – 'long live our father and founder', so loudly that the whole reception hall re-echoed. Many were surprised by this unusual sight and curiosity brought them closer."

From the airport he was taken by car to Staten Island. A bus with Schoenstatt members from Brooklyn arrived after lunch. Many of them had not gone to work that day so that they could see Fr Kentenich and be with him. He went to the entrance of the house and took his stand on

159

a sort of terrace, so that the new arrivals could greet him in turn. Many who had not been able to go to the airport, and who had not been to Milwaukee, were happy to have this opportunity to shake his hand. Although he could not speak their language, Fr Kentenich greeted each one personally. He had a particularly happy knack with the children. One of them, whom he had taken in his arms, was attracted by his long beard and gave it a hearty tug. Fr Kentenich thanked the many who had visited him in Milwaukee, and who had undertaken the twenty hours' bus-drive from New York to do so. He drew their attention to a great gift and grace which God had given the Romance peoples, in particular the Puerto Ricans – an outstandingly childlike spirit. Taking a child by the hand he said: "You should all become inwardly like a child, even if outwardly you have to stand your ground and be as strong as an oak."

In the course of the afternoon he was taken back to Kennedy Airport, from where he set out by Swissair for Rome. Once again the crowd of people and the noise they made attracted the attention of the other passengers. Fr Kentenich remained completely calm. Fr Jaime Salazar remarked on Fr Kentenich's extraordinary capacity to be wholly receptive for others and even to make contact with people who really had nothing to do with him. "I can remember a rather curious gentleman watching us. From his appearance he was an Arab. Fr Kentenich greeted him so warmly that he could do nothing else than return the greeting with equal friendliness, even though he remained totally amazed."

The journey to Rome went off smoothly. As a result of fog the plane was re-routed from Zürich to Geneva. It was after midday that he landed in an Arabian plane at the Leonardo da Vinci Airport in Rome. After taking a break at the Carmelite Convent in the Via Innocenzo X, he announced his arrival at the Pallottine Generalate at the Ponte Sisto towards evening. His appearance gave rise to amazement and confusion. No one had sent a telegram to Milwaukee. Fr Kentenich was just as amazed by this reaction, yet he remained calm.

The following day he dictated a memorandum for the Church authorities in which he briefly gave the course of events. The text reads: ''The facts: The call from the exchange (Western Union) took place on 13 September 1965 towards 5.30 p.m. A woman first asked me for my name and my personal telephone number. She obviously wanted to make sure of my identity. She then told me that a telegram had arrived for me from Rome. I asked, 'Is the wording in German or in English?' The answer was, 'In English. It is worded as follows: In the name of Father General immediately come to Rome. Signed: Burggraf.' I thanked the telephonist and asked her to send written confirmation of the telegram as soon as possible. She agreed to do so. In order that there should be no mistake, the house and street number were checked carefully. However, the telegram was not delivered. On 16 September 1965 I left Milwaukee by air and arrived on the evening of 17 September at the Pallottine Generalate. Fr Möhler, the Superior General, was not there. In his place his secretary, Fr Burggraf, told me with every sign of amazement and shock that he knew nothing of such a telegram. It had, at any rate, not been written or sent off by him.''

The news of Fr Kentenich's surprising appearance in

Rome spread like wildfire to those who knew of his case. He had been expected in October, and this at the invitation of the Holy Office. And then all of a sudden he was there, summoned by a telegram which he stated he had personally received, but which no one had sent off. The Cardinals of the Holy Office were surprised and amazed by his presence, and eventually they became very angry. The patient diplomatic work of the past months seemed to have been suddenly and completely destroyed. The plenary session of the Cardinals of the Holy Office decided on 24 September that Fr Kentenich had to return to Milwaukee. One of the consultors, a friend of Schoenstatt, Cardinal Bea, tried to find a way to at best put off the return journey. During a discussion with Fr Kentenich he asked whether, in view of Fr Kentenich's advanced age, another journey over the Atlantic would not cause his health to suffer. Fr Kentenich replied that he felt in the best of health and could set out on the return journey at any time, as soon as the Cardinals desired it.

The tension surrounding Fr Kentenich remained unabated in the days and weeks that followed. (He himself remained calm and ate and slept quite normally.) Informed circles in Rome considered, discussed and argued the pros and cons for his remaining in Rome. A German bishop, who visited him almost daily at the time, related later, "In all those difficult months he never once, not even by the least negative remark, said anything about his opponents. He always treated them and their attitude to him objectively and tried to understand their position. At the same time he equally upheld his mission without any false compromise. In the pro-

162

cess he never made the least attempt to achieve anything by dubious means. He acted according to the principle: The truth will set you free! Humanly speaking those were very difficult weeks in which everything was at stake. In the midst of these storms his hope remained unshaken.''

"You will see," he said to a trusted collaborator, "things will turn out alright. Our Lady will be victorious. I have been through greater storms, and our Lady has always been victorious." On 20 October, at a plenary session of the Cardinals of the Holy Office, the decision was taken that Fr Kentenich did not have to return to Milwaukee. His case was transferred, as had already been done with Schoenstatt as a whole, to the jurisdiction of the Congregation for Religious and all the decrees that had limited him until then were consequently cancelled. Two days later Pope Paul VI confirmed the decision of the Cardinals: Fr Kentenich was free. Bishop Tenhumberg, Auxiliary Bishop of Münster, was allowed to pass on this news to him that same day. "When I told him the news that the plenary session of the Cardinals of the Holy Office had removed all restrictions from him, he looked at me and was silent for a time. I had the impression that he was praying. Then he asked me very simply to tell him more details.'' He received the news on exactly the same day as he had set out for exile fourteen years before (he had had to leave Schoenstatt on 22 October 1951). He himself later interpreted these years as the fourteen Stations of the Cross he had had to go.

Meanwhile the fourth and final session of the Second Vatican Council was in progress in Rome. Two thousand five hundred bishops from all over the world were working on the final documents. This offered Fr Kentenich a welcome opportunity once again to pick up personal contact with bishops from various parts of the world, in particular with those bishops in whose dioceses the Schoenstatt Movement had taken root. Archbishop Adolfo Tortolo, of Paraná, Argentina, received him on a number of occasions at his residence in 55 Via Mascherone. "His first words at his first visit were words of thanks to me. Gratefulness characterised his greatness of soul, which had been tested and purified. He did not speak about the past years he had suffered through. He spoke with admirable calm about his favourite dogma; about God the Father in heaven and his Providence. These were not just concepts to him, they were experiences that filled him inwardly." At his second visit they spoke about celibacy (which was a hotly debated topic at that time). Archbishop Tortolo has kept one sentence very particularly in mind, because it gave him much food for thought. Fr Kentenich had said, "Whoever does not live as a child before the heavenly Father is an orphan. Celibacy will always be hard for him, indeed impossible." At their third meeting "we spoke about our Lady and about his proposed visit to our country. He spoke with great enthusiasm about the Argentine."

Since he was now able to move about freely, Fr Kentenich left the Pallottine Generalate and moved to the house of the Mainz Sisters of Providence (today St John Eudes), which was situated somewhat outside of Rome. From then on he was surrounded by his sons and daughters who had hastened to join him from Germany, South America, Australia and South Africa. Visits from bishops and other members of the hierarchy were the order of the day. There were letters, each day great piles of them, and constant telephone calls. Throughout these weeks Fr Kentenich had little time to sleep, at most he got a few hours every night. He was radiant with joy that could be almost tangibly felt. He was wholly there for whoever came to him. Antoinette Furtado from India (who had completed her studies in Social Science), had known Schoenstatt since 1960. What had impressed her most was the message of God's fatherhood, a God who loves us, not because we have deserved it, but because he is our Father and we are his children. On the first evening after her arrival in Rome, on 4 December, she met Fr Kentenich for the first time. "I felt like a child towards him and this expression alone justified my own feelings. I had met my father." Each day Fr Kentenich gave talks for the leaders of the Schoenstatt Family. "What he placed before us came as though from a full barrel after the tap had been opened," commented one of the participants. He celebrated his eightieth birthday on 16 November. The day began with the celebration of the Eucharist in the house chapel; Fr Kentenich was the main celebrant. Bishop Bolte, Auxiliary Bishop Tenhumberg and Bishop Antonio Plaza of the Argentine were present in the sanctuary. After Holy Mass the congratulatory reception began in the big hall in the left wing of the house. Midday soon arrived. The dining room had been festively decorated for the occasion. As usual, there were speeches during the meal. "The climax came with the dessert," relates Cecilia Höltschi, a German teacher in Rome, "when a giant cake with eighty burning candles was brought in. There was a chorus of Oh's and Ah's!

in the light of faith, but also in the light of evolution, and, on the other hand, it must be seen in the light of Church teaching, in the light of God's plan. It is and remains the eternal plan of the eternal God that the Church will not be born, will not be conceived anew, and cannot be completed, without the Mother of God.''

On 13 December he wrote a Christmas Letter to the whole Schoenstatt Family from Rome. In it he tried to summarise the fruits that had been reaped from the long years of his exile. God's great gift to the family was the new image of the Father, the new image of the child, and the new image of the community. Fr Kentenich had always taught that God is Love; what was new was the way in which God's merciful love was particularly strongly stressed. The new image of the child of God was that of the miserable child who was on that account worthy of mercy. This by no means neglects the reality of one's personal merits and co-operation with grace, but our special attention should be drawn to God's love, to his infinite, merciful love for us. The feast of Christmas was approaching. The Schoenstatt Family was waiting longingly for Fr Kentenich to return home to Schoenstatt after the fourteen years of his exile, and to celebrate Midnight Mass in the original shrine. Negotiations had started in Rome to this end, but time passed and no results were made known. Finally, on 22 December Fr Kentenich was granted an audience with Pope Paul VI. In a brief speech the Holy Father thanked him for all he had done for the Church.

For his part Fr Kentenich promised to co-operate with the Schoenstatt Family in carrying out the great post-Conciliar mission of the Church. He presented a chalice

167

to the Pope as a gift for the church that was to be built in honour of Mary, Mother of the Church. A photograph by Felici shows Fr Kentenich standing before the Pope, humble yet erect, with the chalice in hand. This meeting closed one epoch and opened the next. Two days later, on 24 December, Fr Kentenich was allowed to travel to Schoenstatt in order to celebrate Midnight Mass in the shrine. No Schoenstatt member wanted to be left behind in Rome. All wanted to fly with him in order to be present at this historic moment of his homecoming. The Sisters of Mary, although they had had no security for doing so, but simply in the faith that he would go home, had reserved half a plane on the flight from Rome to Frankfurt. ''The Miracle of the Holy Night'', that is, the freedom of Schoenstatt's father and founder, the undoing of his fetters, had become a reality.

What thoughts may have gone through his soul as he flew towards Schoenstatt after an absence of fourteen years? How many memories, how many people, how much joy and suffering, may he not have borne in his heart? ''When I floated over the clouds like that, when I hovered over the sea,'' he remarked later, ''I liked to think of St Augustine who at his time travelled similar ways from Tagaste as I was then flying, although in the opposite direction... During this return journey here I liked to think of St Paul as well. It was his favourite occupation to look as deeply as possible into the plans of God, the Eternal Father.'' A large crowd of Schoenstatt members met him at Frankfurt airport. They accompanied him in a procession of cars to Schoenstatt. On the way he paid a brief visit to the Pallottine Provincial in Limburg. They then continued on their way to

Schoenstatt. Fr Kentenich got out of the car and first made for the original shrine. The whole valley was filled with a strange atmosphere that evening, the Vigil of Christmas. Fr Kentenich was returning after fourteen years of exile, he, the instrument who had proclaimed Schoenstatt's message to the world; a man was returning, an eighty-year-old priest, who after most severe trials was able to greet his heavenly Mother once again – calmly, unharmed, strong and victorious. (''Father will be taking a few journeys, he will fight a few battles. Then he will come home again, crowned with victory'' – that is how he knelt there.) A fortunate snapshot has captured this moment when Fr Kentenich knelt praying in the shrine. The depth and inner calm of his gaze, his upright bearing, his hands folded in prayer, express what cannot be put into words.

Word had gone round that the reunion of the father with his whole Family would take place at 6 p.m. in the 'Marienschule', the high school conducted by the Sisters of Mary. There was an air of amazement, joy, and eager expectancy. Tears of joy filled many eyes. Fr Kentenich slowly climbed the steps to reach the microphone. ''Our Lady is giving me the Family once more; it has, of course, always lived in my heart, but she is placing it back in my hands so that I can form and mould it in the way corresponding somewhat to the plans of eternal Truth, and so that I may then pass over into eternity where I shall continue to guide my life-work in a new way.'' Some people felt sorry for him, because they saw what an effort it had been for him to climb the steps to the stage; they thought of the weight of his advanced years. When someone told him of this, he replied with a smile, ''Oh,

13. IN THE LIGHT OF VICTORY

For Fr Kentenich Christmas 1965 meant the start of a time of carrying an extraordinary burden of work. Now that the fourteen years of exile were over everyone wanted to see him, to speak to him, to hear a personal word from him, or at least shake his hand. So it wasn't easy to get near him. Four Sisters of Mary served as his secretaries in order to cope with the most varied spheres of his work. He continued to stand as before for his talks, and he was always faced with a battery of microphones and tape recorders. He spoke without notes – his words simply flowed. Despite his age and the suffering of his exile he was as he had always been. His hair and beard had turned completely white, but the radiance of his eyes had grown. He was like a great river flowing deeply and calmly by, at whose waters everyone who wanted could slake their thirst. There was no trace of bitterness. Signs of tiredness and old age could not be found. At the end of March 1966 he gave his blessing to a group of the Women's League at the conclusion of a training course on Mount Schoenstatt. When they had said "Amen" he added with a smile, "I don't look as though I have come out of exile, do I? There are people who simply need such air, and they flourish best in it."

Fr August Ziegler from Switzerland had not spoken personally to Fr Kentenich for many years. So early in 1966 he set off for Schoenstatt. He hoped to meet him privately, but he had to wait for him along with many others in the "Schulungsheim", the Training Centre of the Sisters of Mary on Mount Schoenstatt, where Fr Kentenich was staying. He saw Fr Kentenich coming down a long passage between two rows of Sisters of Mary. ''As he gradually drew nearer, he seemed to me like a being from another world, as though he was returning from a visit to heaven. Of course, he looked older than when I had known him at Fribourg. But that was by no means what impressed me most. No, it was rather a strange transfiguration which radiated from him, a state of being permeated by heavenly peace, by heavenly joy and kindness.''

On his way to Schoenstatt Fr Ziegler had drawn up a list of questions he had wanted to discuss with Fr Kentenich. But once he was with him he left these problems aside and related what interested him personally. ''Some problems seemed to me to be solved merely by his renewed presence in the midst of his own. His presence seemed to me to be a pledge for the presence and activity of God in this world and in people's lives.''

Besides giving himself unreservedly to the sons and daughters of his family, Fr Kentenich tried to set up contact with the German bishops. In February 1966 he wrote them a letter in which he told them of his intention and readiness to co-operate with them, the shepherds of the People of God, in the realization of the post-Conciliar mission of the Church. In March he spent a whole day with Bishop Höffner of Münster and discussed pastoral and social problems with him. In the afternoon of 9 May he visited the Bishop of Treves, Dr Matthias Wehr, accompanied by Bishop Tenhumberg. It was already dark as they set off on the return journey to Schoenstatt and crossed the Rhine Bridge at Coblenz. The driver was not acquainted with the area and at a turning was hit by an oncoming car. The jolt was so great that both Fr

Kentenich and Bishop Tenhumberg received head and body injuries although they both wore safety belts. They were taken as quickly as possible by ambulance to St Josef's Hospital in Coblenz. On their arrival, Fr Kentenich saw to it that the bishop was cared for first. They spent the night in hospital. They had got off lightly. As a result of the bruising Fr Kentenich suffered great pain for a few days and could not move his arms properly. For the rest, the accident had no further consequences. "In the past the faithful were sprinkled with the blood of bulls and goats," Fr Kentenich remarked, "but now I have been sprinkled with episcopal blood". Considering his manifold and continuous burden of work his health was very good. He had weak lungs and often had colds with bronchitis, and because he would not spare himself and continued to give talks, it usually took him a long time to recover from a cold. Once, when he again had a cold and could hardly speak, he said jokingly that just on that account he would immediately hold a retreat course, so that he could "speak himself better" and that his voice would return.

A month later he visited Bishop Stimpfle of Augsburg, who had invited him for a concelebration followed by breakfast with some priests. Fr Kentenich expressed the wish that the devotion to Mary and the true fatherliness of the bishop might flourish in the diocese. The bishop answered that it was his aim to make his diocese a Family of God. Then, referring to his visitor, he added, "patriarcha et propheta locutus est" (a patriarch and prophet has spoken). In September Fr Kentenich travelled to Bavaria. There he visited Cardinal Döpfner, Archbishop of Münich and Freising, Bishop Schröffer of Eichstätt and Bishop Graber of Regensburg. In October he was in Münster and concelebrated with Bishop Höffner and Auxiliary Bishop Tenhumberg at a solemn Holy Mass in the ancient cathedral. He also received bishops in Schoenstatt. Towards the end of November, for example, a group of bishops from countries outside Germany came to Schoenstatt. They were shown over the various houses, and then had a meal with Fr Kentenich. "We were amazed," said Auxiliary Bishop Bruno Maldaner of Sao Paulo, "that at his age the founder was so active and so cheerful after all he must have gone through".

He received a number of visits from Cardinal Silva Henriquez, Archbishop of Santiago, Chile; and Cardinal Agnetto Rossi from Brazil turned up on occasion at Schoenstatt.

One of the central themes of his talks was our Lady's great mission for the present era, and in particular her mission from Schoenstatt. He did this at a time when it was not fashionable to preach on Marian topics; when not a few theologians and pastors considered devotion to Mary outdated, or at least not essential for the life of the Church. In May 1966 he could once again celebrate the start of May, Mary's month, with his Family after a break of fourteen years. He encouraged everyone to make every day of the month a day for Mary and hence a day of grace. In a talk to the girls from Würzburg and Cologne he explained what it means to be a "little Mary": "clear head, warm heart, joyful emotions, firm will." And then he showed how this ideal became a reality in our Lady's life. At the end of the month he travelled to Southern Germany, to the Liebfrauenhöhe, for the blessing of the

Crown Church there. As he entered the Church, which was filled to capacity, the people began to clap and sing: "The fetters have fallen". In gratitude for all that our Lady had brought about in the past years, Fr Kentenich wanted the title "Victress" to be added from then on to her title as Mother Thrice Admirable and Queen. This was not improvised on the spur of the moment, but was a title he had long thought over. He answered those who thought the time of devotion to Mary to be long past with a clear and decisive "No". "We know that God's present plan of salvation has essentially depended on the agreement of our Lady, as the representative of mankind. … We take it for granted that the salvation of the coming confused era is also dependent on our Lady's 'Yes'." A parish priest in München had published an article on Mary in a catechetical periodical, the "Katechetischen Blättern". His argument was theologically poor and his position was psychologically untenable. The author went so far as to say that devotion to Mary was merely a substitute for genuine piety. Fr Rudolf Ammann answered this article with a letter to the editor. When Fr Kentenich heard about this he wrote to Fr Ammann and congratulated him on his initiative:

"Schoenstatt, 22.5.67. Carissime! A sincere thank you to you for your dialogue. It is courageous, objectively incontestable, psychologically sympathetic and significant for contemporary history. It would make me happy if it could have an influence not only on our own ranks, but beyond. In our own ranks: all of us together have an outspokenly Marian mission, we have been schooled in Mariology for years, we have garnered rich experience in Marian devotion, and should therefore be prepared to defend the cause of our Lady courageously and reverently when the opportunity offers. We may then be certain that a special blessing will be given to the whole Family and the Church. Therefore once again my sincere congratulations, thanks and all-round encouragement.''

Fr Kentenich considered it most important that devotion to Mary should be based on a solid foundation. So he always tried to take his bearings from the biblical picture of Mary. He also made use of the Church Fathers and the teaching office of the Church. At the same time he included his own personal experience. It is possible to acquire a theoretical foundation by thorough study, but what is far more valuable is to pass on in a living way decades of experience of living in a covenant of love with Mary, a covenant that has proved itself in every storm. In one of his Sunday sermons he drew the attention of the congregation to a principle ''that I have always put into practice personally in all the battles of my life, and that has made it easy for me not to break down''. What was this principle? ''Taking the covenant of love seriously! I am wholly convinced that it is possible to base one's entire life on the covenant of love! I could prove this to you in every circumstance of my life.'' He formulated the same principle on another occasion. On 8 July Bishop Heinrich Tenhumberg ordained three deacons in the house chapel of the ''Schulungsheim'' on Mount Schoenstatt. At the end of Holy Mass, at which he had concelebrated with the bishop, Fr Kentenich spoke briefly. He reminded his listeners of the consecration of the first generation to Mary, when they had placed their hand on the sodality banner and said, ''This is the standard I have chosen, I shall never abandon it,

I swear this to God". He then explained, "We were always of the opinion, because we were so profoundly gripped by the special character of our covenant of love as a mutual covenant, that our Lady at the same time called out to us, as it were, 'This is the instrument I have chosen, I shall never abandon it, I swear this to God!' And if our Lady, the faithful Virgin, has taken an oath on something, she will always remain true to her word."

He always commemorated Mary's feasts with particular solemnity. On these days, a Sister of Mary testified, "he radiated something, like someone coming from the next world". Without doubt his personal relationship to God's Mother was part of his secret; it was the soul of his life. "It is simply a fact," he said on one occasion, "our love for our Lady is so warm that we need only hear some hymn to her for everything in us to be awakened. It is as though everything in the soul sounds and resounds as soon as Mary's name is uttered."

In October 1966 the October Week took place in the school hall of the "Marienschule". Fr Kentenich gave a total of nine talks in these days. He announced three main points for discussion, but he did not get further than the first. One of the participants relates, "We experienced once again the tremendous vitality of our father. With a sovereign smile he exceeded the sixty minutes' time limit, even when the people in the hall began to fidget because they could hardly sit still any longer." The golden thread that can be followed up right through the congress was the conviction "... the past years have set a sure and visible seal on the markedly divine character of our Family". He tried to imprint this believing conviction very deeply on his audience through the talks. The congress ended with a candlelight procession from the shrine in the valley to that of the Sisters of Mary on Mount Schoenstatt. Accompanied by Cardinal Silva Henriquez, Fr Kentenich walked with the procession until about half way up the mountain, then he got into a car and was driven the rest of the way. Two months later a similar great congress took place in Schoenstatt. Fr Kentenich, who was always open for current events ("the great axiom of our family is to offer an answer to the suffering and needs of the era"), had as his aim to anchor his followers in God, in the supernatural world, in the Eternal, the Absolute. However, this by no means meant neglecting the human. On the contrary, his concern was to integrate and elevate the human into the divine. "You may expect to hear nothing else from me until the end of my life than references to the divine, which alone offers us security and a key to the past and future." On 16 July 1967 the Brothers of Mary and the Family Movement celebrated the Silver Jubilee of their foundation. Fr Kentenich visited the former concentration camp at Dachau for this occasion, the first and only time he did so after his release. He said, "I think I should confess openly and honestly that I see it as my God-given task to lead countless people to surrender themselves totally to the eternal, infinite God, to help them to feel at home in the supernatural world and reality".

During the 1967 October Week he gave out as a programme: "We should oppose a world fleeing from God with a world seeking God." Jaime Ochagavia, who was at that time a seminarian belonging to the community of the Schoenstatt Fathers, was able to take part in this congress and in the one that followed in December. Two passages in Fr Kentenich's talks have remained unforgettable to him. The first is a statement about God as the great "You" in our lives. "Fr Kentenich expressed this in the following terms: Above You, below You, before You, behind You, You, You, You, You! While he said this his hand beat time on the podium." The other passage was a quotation from a prayer by Vincent Pallotti: "Not food, but God; not drink, but God; not clothing, but God; not love, but God." "These words penetrated me very deeply, they set their stamp on me. They touched my heart. They re-echoed in me for months and filled my soul. They suddenly popped up again when I was in the middle of a lecture at the university. These words moved something within me. They possessed the power of God."

The man, the priest, who was passionately in love with God and the supernatural world, was at the same time extremely human and approachable. He radiated love, peace and joy. He had a great sense of humour. On one occasion he was handing out chocolates to a group of somewhat older girls. One of them did not want to accept any, saying that she had read that saints gave up such things. "Don't worry, take them," Fr Kentenich told her, "that doesn't apply to you". On another occasion, after a consecration in the shrine, he handed out pictures. Some of them were photos of himself. With a smile he remarked, "That is not me, but my work". On yet another occasion he was talking to older members of the Women's Union. One of them was 93, another 82. He joked, "I have been outdone. But one day I want to be the oldest". In order to end a discussion with a Sister of

Mary he used to say, " … benedicat Virgo Maria," and expected the reply, "Of course" from her. Once a sister was trying to get him to come to a meeting of her course. Humanly speaking it was very difficult to achieve this. What was she to do? She suddenly got an original idea. While she was presenting her petition to Fr Kentenich, she unexpectedly interrupted the conversation with the words "benedicat Virgo Maria". "Of course," Fr Kentenich responded like a shot. She had got what she wanted.

He laughed with those who laughed and wept with those who wept. Sometimes it was possible to see that he was in a good mood. If he received sad news, or if someone had entrusted a difficult problem to him, it was not unusual to see this mirrored in his face. During a telephone conversation he often closed his eyes in order to be wholly concentrated on the person at the other end of the line. When someone wanted to spare him suffering, and so told him only what was positive, withholding the negative, he said that in principle this attitude was good, but "father has a right to his children's tears". He possessed the charism of accepting and relating to people very personally. Whoever came to him felt completely understood and highly valued. He was once asked why people had such a sense of well-being when they saw him. "That is father's secret," he replied. "He lets each person be himself, he accepts and takes up each person as he is." Ernesto Livacic, at that time Chile's representative to Unesco, visited him on 15 November 1966 in Schoenstatt. He recalls this meeting: "It was a winter's evening after a full working day for Fr Kentenich. He was completely receptive, completely father. I had expected that on account of tiredness and Fr Kentenich's many responsibilities, our conversation would be brief. Strangely enough it took much longer than planned. And at the end he said that he greatly regretted that I had only come to Schoenstatt for that one day, and that we could therefore not have a longer conversation. He invited me to come again and to plan for a longer stay. Before I said goodbye, he went into an adjoining room and brought me a few presents: some rosaries (that is for the soul), and then with the words 'that is for the body' a bottle of Rhine wine. After a few photos had been taken he accompanied me to the door. He waved for a long time, till the car taking me to Coblenz station had disappeared from view.''

Towards the end of 1967 his health began to fail. His pace of work was simply exhausting. At times one saw how tired he was and his face was very pale. He usually said nothing about his health. When the Brothers of Mary asked him early in August for a meeting, he answered that under the circumstances at that time it was ''metaphysically impossible'' for him to find time for it. He conducted retreats for the sisters on Mount Schoenstatt, he had to attend a meeting of the leaders of the Institute of Our Lady of Schoenstatt at Haus Regina, a congress for priests was taking place at Metternich and they insisted on seeing him. He had other engagements outside Schoenstatt; from 22 to 25 August he had to conduct a retreat for the students of the Schoenstatt Fathers in Münster, from 3 to 4 September he was visiting Oberkirch. In addition to this, the General Chapter of the Sisters of Mary was starting on 8 September. Someone in Schoenstatt commented about this time: "Everybody seems to be making their holiday here. Fr Kentenich seems to recover while he works." Then followed the October Week. During the Christmas Congress it was evident that he was not well. And yet he kept up his pace of work if at all possible. On the evening of 30 April 1968 the Schoenstatt Family had a candlelight procession on Mount Schoenstatt and then gathered at the back of the "Schulungsheim" with the obvious intention to get Fr Kentenich to speak. To everyone's joy the window of his office opened. He reached out both hands to the crowd standing with burning red lanterns under his window and looking up expectantly to him. On account of the chill in the air he was wearing a biretta, and in the course of his address he withdrew slightly into the room. Yet his voice came clearly and unmistakably through the microphone and loudspeaker. He spoke for about 45 minutes, giving orientation and inspiration for the month of May that was about to begin. "One reason why the world and Church are shaken by revolutions," he said, "is because the people belonging to the Church to a large extent do not want to pay tribute to our Lady's triumph in the way she deserves. People no longer want to accept our Lady's mission to create order in the present-day world. This is obviously the work of the devil, who is brilliantly able to force our Lady, the Woman who tramples on the serpent, into the background, and to ensure that all sorts of ideas are cultivated in place of our Lady's mission." During this month Fr Kentenich had someone read to him every day about our Lady. This lasted at least fifteen minutes, "although he was often very tired," one of his secretaries relates.

182

On 9 June 1968, the church dedicated to the Blessed Trinity for perpetual adoration on Mount Schoenstatt was solemnly blessed. This fulfilled a promise made by the Sisters of Mary during the Second World War and the Dachau years. Fr Kentenich was too ill to attend. In a letter that was read out to the people attending the ceremony, he gave expression to his hope for the future. "... that our Schoenstatt Family may become even more than until now a most perfect possible colony of heaven and a universally creative castle of God."

His health could no longer stand the pace. He had heart trouble. Hardly had he recovered slightly than he was again at the service of all who visited him and needed him. In August Mrs Olga Rist de Kast was able to attend Holy Mass which he celebrated in the shrine behind Haus Regina. She related later, "He looked old and tired as he walked uprightly and reverently to the altar; but when he began to speak (and he spoke for almost an hour) his face lit up; suddenly he was another person, a young man. His way of speaking was so attractive, so uplifting and clear."

The Kintscher family, together with other families, visited him on 28 August in the "Schulungsheim". "But this is a biblical group for once," he greeted them with a smile. When they asked him for orientation and directives, he replied, "On the whole it is true to say today that people are tired and stale. This is often the case especially with the clergy. People are simply afraid: How will things end? ... We are conquering the world, and we are doing so because our Lady has chosen us to be her instruments; and she will continue to do so. And then secondly: The salvation of the world is dependent on the renewal of the family alone." In conclusion: "You should take home with you the deep conviction that our Lady wants to use us as instruments to create a new world and to lead the Church to the shores of a new era. And that is what I wish you all, and I also wish it to myself with all my heart."

At the beginning of September Claudio Giminez of Paraguay, a seminarian belonging to the community of the Schoenstatt Fathers, arranged for two Irish seminarians to meet Fr Kentenich. They proposed to attend his Holy Mass. "On the agreed day," Father Claudio recalls, "when I fetched the two, I went past the Marienau where Fr Kentenich was staying just then. Without really thinking I involuntarily looked upwards. Fr Kentenich was watching me from a balcony and greeted me with a smile and a wave. I called up to him, 'We will be there in a moment.' He replied loudly, 'Good.' I went with my Irish friends to the sacristy. Fr Kentenich greeted us respectfully and asked, 'Should I say Mass in Latin or in English?' The two were quite satisfied with Latin, so he said the Mass in Latin."

Representatives of the Schoenstatt Family gathered in Essen for the "Katholikentag". On 7 September Fr Kentenich wrote a long letter to them in which he enlarged on our Lady's mission for our present-day world. He made the statement: "We are living in Apocalyptic times." This did not mean that he thought the end of the world was at hand, but bore witness to the fact "... that the post-modern age is similar to the end of the world in a way that is unique until now – they are almost as like as two peas in a pod". It is impossible to explain such times with purely human criteria. The intellectual-spiritual controversy shaking the world and Church has to be traced back to a gigantic battle between divine and diabolical powers. "The powers of God and Satan have chosen the world as their battlefield, and through their instruments they fight for world dominion. This obviously occurs today to an extraordinary degree. This is how in the light of faith, we can understand the present state of affairs." Our Lady's mission in the spiritual battles of our days is already indicated: "As the chosen instrument in the hand of the living God she has been given the task, as the official and permanent helpmate and associate of our Lord in the entire work of redemption, and in connection with him, to crush the head of Satan, so that finally the world will again become God's possession and offer him the honour due to him."

The feast of the Holy Name of Mary was celebrated on 12 September. Fr Kentenich gave a talk that made a deep impression on the congregation. "It must be and remain our task to introduce our Lady into the battles of the present-day world and Church, and see to it that Mary again receives the place due to her according to the Eternal Father's plan. Mary is part of the redemption and governing of the world. She has the task to lead Christ into the world and the world to Christ. We are convinced that the great crises of the present era cannot be overcome without Mary." After this talk a Sister of Mary went to him and said, "Father, you must love our Lady a lot in order to be able to say such nice things about her". He replied joyfully: "It is true, I love her very much..."

14. THE RETURN HOME TO THE FATHER

Schoenstatt, Sunday 15 September 1968. On the heights of Mount Schoenstatt, the bells were ringing the Angelus. A large number of Sisters of Mary slowly and silently gathered from various directions in the Adoration Church. It was a special day. The Sisters of the Providentia Province were celebrating their provincial superior's feast day. Fr Kentenich wanted to give them joy, so he was celebrating Holy Mass with them for the first time at this place. After Holy Mass they were invited to go down to the auditorium under the church where he wanted to address them. Shortly after 6 a.m. Fr Kentenich left his room in the ''Schulungsheim''. Two Sisters of Mary were waiting for him with a car that was to drive him to the Adoration Church. He was recollected, pale, calm. He seemed borne by silent joy. Along the short way from the ''Schulungsheim'' to the church (about three hundred meters) he was greeted by sisters going there on foot. Fr Kentenich waved to them. Everything happened normally, as on so many Sundays in Schoenstatt. Who could have foreseen that this was the last stretch of the way on Fr Kentenich's earthly pilgrimage? Had he himself had a premonition of it? What may he have felt at that moment? Surely joy, because he could celebrate Holy Mass on Sunday, the Lord's day, on which the Church commemorated Christ's resurrection in a special way. A special joy, because it was one of Mary's feast-days, the day of her Seven Sorrows (although the Sunday texts would be used in the Liturgy as prescribed). The special joy, because he could celebrate the Eucharist for the first time in this church promised to our Lady in the Dachau period.

It is probable that at this moment Fr Kentenich was not thinking of death, although death was not strange and unknown to him. How often it had been close to him, how often he had confronted himself with it. He had prepared himself for this hour: when he had been given up by the doctors in Engers; in the concentration camp; on the many occasions when he had staked his life. In Dachau he had written in a prayer: ''May I, with zeal, proclaim you to all peoples and daily dare to fight for you with courage, so that your kingdom triumphs everywhere and reaches to the ends of all the earth.'' He had taught his followers to prepare daily for that moment. He was well able to say with Paul: ''I die every day'', because throughout his life he had borne ''the death pangs of Jesus Christ'' in his own body (cf. 2 Cor 4,10). The day's Mass had been continued in his life's Mass. On more than one occasion he had told Fr Menningen confidentially, ''I shall die in harness,'' anticipating that his death would come suddenly. It is possible that his words on 8 December 1944 in Dachau were a valid proclamation of his own death. "And if in his wise Providence God suddenly sends the angel of death to us to transplant us into another world in which he will reveal his plans to us, we hope that in close connection with all our loved ones we may be able to be and do more for Schoenstatt than while here on earth.''

The car came to a halt in front of the Adoration Church. Fr Kentenich climbed the steps to the square in front of the church and for some moments watched the fountain which, with its flowing waters, symbolises the seven

187

sacraments. In the sacristy he quietly greeted the sacristan and Fr Weigand, asking the latter if he had had a good rest during his holiday, which he had just completed. Then he vested, and punctually at 6.15 a.m. approached the altar. They were joined during the opening rite by Fr Drago, a young Carmelite from Yugoslavia. Fr Kentenich celebrated the Mass of the Fifteenth Sunday after Pentecost in Latin. In the light of what was to happen, the readings have a prophetic ring: "As long as we still have time, let us all do good," the Apostle Paul admonishes us. At the consecration Fr Kentenich genuflected to the ground even though it cost him great effort. He distributed Holy Communion with the other two priests. At the end he gave his priestly blessing and concluded with the "Ite missa est". He bowed deeply before the tabernacle and returned to the sacristy. It was almost 7 a.m. In the sacristy Fr Kentenich unvested, greeted Fr Drago and invited both priests to lunch. The sacristan had placed a prie-dieu next to the table. Fr Kentenich took note of this but remained standing at the table. The sister placed a small parcel of rosaries in front of him for his blessing. He took off his glasses, blessed the rosaries, placed his hands on the table and stood like this for a few moments. "We were under the impression," related Fr Weigand, "that Fr Kentenich was making his thanksgiving for the Holy Mass he had celebrated". Without a special thought, Fr Weigand looked at his watch. It was just after 7 a.m.

Suddenly Fr Kentenich fell forwards onto the table. He tried to hold himself up with his hands. This prevented him from hitting his face. Fr Weigand and Fr Drago, who were standing near him, immediately supported him under his arms and tried to hold him. But they couldn't manage, he was too heavy for them. They tried to help him onto a chair, but this didn't work either. No other choice was left to them than to let him slip slowly to the floor. The two priests supported his head until the sister had brought a cushion. As Fr Weigand let go of Fr Kentenich's left arm, the latter instinctively reached for his heart. He breathed normally for one or two minutes. Fr Weigand gave him general absolution and asked for the holy oils for the anointing of the sick. There was a pause, then Fr Kentenich took two deep breaths, after that no sign of life remained. It was 7.07 a.m. Meanwhile the doctor had been called. Dr Steinkamp arrived at 7.15 a.m., went up to Fr Kentenich immediately, listened to his heart and said to those present, "His heart has stopped beating".

The news of Fr Kentenich's sudden death spread like wild-fire through the whole Schoenstatt Family inside and outside Germany. The mass media in Germany paid tribute to him and his work. The radio reported his death that same day. His picture was shown on television the following day. Various newspapers (Frankfurter Allgemeine, Deutsche Tagespost, Rheinischer Merkur and others) published articles on his life. "Father Joseph Kentenich," the Deutsche Tagespost reported, "was able to brave every difficulty because he was wholly a man who trusted in God and personally lived what he encouraged others to do in his rich life". A telegram from the Holy Father, Pope Paul VI, arrived from the Vatican: "The Holy Father conveys his sincere sympathy and assurance of prayer at the death of Fr Kentenich, highly deserving Founder of the Schoenstatt Movement.

Cardinal Cicognani.'' A number of the hierarchy sent letters of sympathy. When Cardinal Frings of Cologne was informed by telephone of Fr Kentenich's death, he remarked: "What a beautiful death for a priest''. Other representatives of the hierarchy sent letters of condolence:

''I am confident that before God's throne he will now watch with fatherly love over that work for which he suffered so much during his earthly pilgrimage...''

A. CARDINAL OTTAVIANI

''His holiness, filled with deep pain by the news of the death of Fr Kentenich, the founder of Schoenstatt, wishes to express his sympathy to your Excellency, the General Praesidium, the Institutes and all Schoenstatt members, at the death of your beloved father and teacher, who was truly great, generous and a genius in his love for the Church. It will be our blessing to remember him, and the memory of his radiant virtues will always inspire us to do good and preserve the right attitude. From heaven may he protect his own and those who knew and esteemed him! Sit in pace locus eius, et habitatio eius in Sancto Sion.''

MONS. GUISEPPE DE TON, *Secretary for the Latin Letters of His Holiness*

''Here the life of a priest has been completed who achieved great things for the Church.''

JULIUS CARDINAL DÖPFNER

''I valued Fr Kentenich highly as a person and priest and great founder of important apostolic works, and will always preserve the best memories of him. I am happy that I could contribute a little to the ending of the injustice done to him. I hope that in him we will all have an intercessor in heaven, and I would like to believe that he hardly needs our poor prayers…''

BRUNO M. HEIM, *Archbishop; Apostolic Delegate to Scandinavia; Apostolic Pronuncio to Finland*

''I only knew him personally for a very short time, but I know more about his work and his suffering. In my opinion the Church has lost a very brave son in him!''

JOSEF CORDEIRO, *Archbishop of Karachi (Pakistan)*

''At the time that Fr Kentenich visited South Africa in 1948, I was parish priest of the Cathedral Parish in Cape Town and chaplain to the Sisters of Mary in Villa Maria. I am, therefore, one of the few lucky ones who had the opportunity to get to know Fr Kentenich personally . . . What impressed me most was the outstanding way he pursued his aim. If one spoke to him about things that moved him particularly, about the renewal of the world in Christ, he did not get tired of speaking about it. If the conversation turned to other things, he would listen patiently and attentively, but his heart was not in it. I can clearly remember how he once said to me: 'Paratus sum ad omnia sacrificia' – I am ready for every sacrifice. What he meant was that all the pleasures, rest, entertainment, etc., which many had planned for him, meant nothing to him . . .''

JOHN C. GARNER, *Archbishop of Pretoria (South Africa)*

''Many were inspired with the spirit of the Gospel by his

191

teaching, and this long before the Vatican Council proclaimed its teaching to the whole world. I myself asked Fr J. Kentenich for guidance, and in him I found one of the greatest men I have ever met. He possessed a great love for God, whose image as Father he portrayed so graphically to everyone through his whole being.''

J. JOBST, *Bishop of Broom, Western Australia*

''The death of their father, who spent his life for his Family, is a painful loss for all the sons and daughters of the large Schoenstatt Family. The work of this charismatic personality has left deep traces on the history of the Church. Our Lady will have been with the departed in his last hour.''

H.H. WITTLER, *Bishop of Osnabrück*

''The unexpected loss of Fr Kentenich has touched me deeply. A saint has died. In these hours of sadness I console myself with two statements I have never forgotten. The first was made to me by Fr Kentenich in Rome on 7 October 1965, 'I am always happy in Our Lady's hands'. He made the second to me in Schoenstatt at the beginning of July 1968, 'Our Lady has done great things for me'. Let us all take consolation in these words.''

GIOVANNI BORTOLASO, *S.J., La Civiltà Cattolica, Rome*

''The news of the death of Fr Kentenich, my longstanding fellow prisoner in Dachau, has moved me greatly. In very truth 'he loved the Church' and gave us – including myself, a Protestant pastor – an example that love for the Church cannot be a 'Platonic love', but always demands our most personal commitment, even to the readiness to suffer for the sake of the Church.''

CHRISTIAN REGER, *former prisoner 26661, Dachau*

"In the difficult time of imprisonment in Dachau, Fr Kentenich was an example to us as a priest and a man."

H. HENNEKENS, PASTOR. *Valkenburg, Holland*

"By his way of life the departed always made a deep impression on me – we arrived on the same day in the concentration camp at Dachau – and his genuinely priestly life and work, even in those 'dark times', will always remain engraved on my memory. His exemplary devotion to Mary in word and deed will certainly have become a pledge to him of heaven."

FRA. RAPHAEL TIJHUIS, *O. Carm*

"Allow me to add that in the past and also after Fr Kentenich's return from exile I personally received extraordinarily valuable inspirations from him, and I feel very closely connected to him and his work. I hope that on some other occasion I may be able to show what the spiritual world of this Father of the Faith has meant and will also in future mean to our task as psychotherapists."

DR FRANZ RUDOLF FABER, *Medical Superintendent, Clemens August Clinic, Neuenkirchen, Oldenburg*

"The hour has come when the just Judge will crown his faithful servant. And next to him is Mary in her wonderful reality. Like all the saints, Fr Kentenich had a big heart, as sensitive and warm as few are. I know that he will now remember me and pray for me. I personally owe him a great deal."

A. TORTOLO, *Archbishop of Paraná, Argentina*

"In the last twenty years I was often with him. Just a few

months ago I had a long conversation with him in Schoenstatt. I admired this eighty-two year old ancient for the power of his thought, his mental clarity, his fantastic memory, his calm, his inner peace, his conviction that the Holy Spirit and the Virgin Mary supported his work, and finally his fine sense of humour, which gave his dignified figure as prophet, and we can even say as martyr, a human dimension.''

BERNARDINO PINERA, Bishop of Temuco, Chile

In the days that followed, Fr Kentenich's body lay in state in the Adoration Church. There were always people praying there. His coffin was placed in front of the altar at which he had celebrated his last Holy Mass. On a small table before the coffin, lay a stole and a chalice. The coffin was surrounded by many white lilies and red roses. Some crowns adorned the altar steps. Thousands passed by to pay their last respects and to take leave of him. Someone later testified: ''It was touching to see the traces of deep sadness in so many faces, the expression of deep love for their father. This pain was not destructive, to some extent it was a transfigured pain.'' Early in the morning of 20 September, at about 2 a.m., the International Schoenstatt Family took leave of him. Men and women from twenty-four countries, representatives of the Schoenstatt Family, expressed themselves in their mother tongue. There were prayers in German, Spanish, English, French, Portuguese, Polish, etc.

8 a.m. The heavens were heavy with cloud, from time to time a fine drizzle fell. The coffin was taken from the Adoration Church to the original shrine. One stop on the way was made in the shrine on Mount Schoenstatt,

where he had so often celebrated Holy Mass after his exile, the last occasion being 12 September. Although it was a working day, about four thousand people were waiting down in the valley, silently or praying the rosary. Before Fr Kentenich found his last resting place in the Church of the Blessed Trinity – symbol of the place to which he ultimately wanted to lead the peoples and nations – he was borne for the last time to the little shrine in the valley.

It was from here that everything had proceeded since that memorable 18 October 1914. Passages from the Founding Document were read out. In the light of all that had happened in 54 years (1914 to 1968), the words of that time resounded with prophetic force: ''When Peter saw God's glory on Tabor, he called out in delight, 'It is good for us to be here. Let us build three tents here!' These words come again and again to my mind. And I have asked myself repeatedly already: would it not be possible for our Sodality chapel to become at the same time our Tabor where Mary's glories are revealed? Without doubt we cannot carry out a greater apostolic deed, or leave our successors a more precious legacy, than to prevail upon our Queen and Sovereign to set up her throne here in a special way, to distribute her treasures and work miracles of grace. You can guess what I am aiming at. I want to make this place a place of pilgrimage, a place of grace, for our house and the whole German Province, perhaps even further afield.''

At about 10 a.m. the coffin left the original shrine, and to the accompaniment of the tolling of bells the procession began to form. A few thousand people walked in procession up Mount Schoenstatt, among them over two hundred priests and about one thousand five hundred Sisters of Mary. On the way hymns of the Schoenstatt Family were sung, some of them in parts. At times the singing clashed and created unusual chords. Once the procession had reached the sisters' cemetery, it branched off the road to the right and passed the sisters' novitiate on the way to the Adoration Church.

The great funeral Mass began after 11 a.m. The church was filled to capacity and many had to remain standing outside. The main celebrant was Bishop Stein of Treves, next to him at the altar stood Bishop Tenhumberg and the Auxiliary Bishop of Aachen. They concelebrated with Monsignor Wissing, Fr Menningen and other priests. Monsignor Bafile, Apostolic Nuncio to Germany, was kneeling in the sanctuary. Holy Mass was solemn and deeply moving. The choir of the Sisters of Mary sang. Bishop Tenhumberg gave the homily after the Gospel.

He reminded his listeners that every great person is a letter from God to his time, a message to us. Our letter from God was the life of our father, the founder of Schoenstatt. He wanted to enlarge on three main chapters out of this letter or book from God: 1) Our God is a God of life, a living God; 2) Our covenant of love with the Mother Thrice Admirable and Queen of Schoenstatt; 3) A word about the mission of the Church for the post-modern era and about Schoenstatt's mission for the Church in this era.

"I have never met a person," he said, "about whom I have been so convinced that at every moment he was listening and attentive to God, and who was, therefore, in the deepest sense an obedient person". The dearest

wish of his heart had been that his work should receive the Church's blessing and be sent out on its mission by her; he had spent his life for her and her mission – very particularly for what lay ahead. But what would this Church say of him one day? "Our lives will decide what the Church will one day say of our father and founder," Bishop Tenhumberg continued. "What is decisive is how we read the letter from God, which he wanted to be, and how we answer it." Then, referring to Schoenstatt's mission, he went on to say, "In my last conversation with him, a telephone call on the eve of his death, he told me that he considered it a loving sign from Divine Providence that present-day historians generally allow that the latest epoch in history began with the outbreak of the First World War, because the Apostolic Movement of Schoenstatt had also been taken into service by God just after the outbreak of that world war. So this work, this work of God, would have a task to fulfil in the Church, with the Church and for the Church in this new epoch." After Holy Mass the coffin was carried to its tomb. The choir sang, "May the angels accompany you to Paradise, may the martyrs greet you at your arrival and lead you to the holy city, Jerusalem."
After the closing prayers and the blessing, all present joined in singing the Salve Regina:

"Hail, holy Queen,
Mother of mercy,
hail, our life, our sweetness
and our hope…"

Fr Kentenich's mortal remains rest in a tomb made of

15. POSTSCRIPT

More than ten years have passed since Fr Kentenich's death. The former sacristy of the Adoration Church on Mount Schoenstatt has been transformed into a sacred place. Men and women, old and young, families, bishops and the simple faithful, intellectuals and workers, all come on pilgrimage to Fr Kentenich's grave. They come from all over Germany and the most varied countries of the world. When you enter the small room, you generally see people there praying or meditating. In all probability they are not so much praying for him as to him, to ask him to intercede for them with God and Our Lady. Holy Mass has already been said countless times at his grave. The novena, "Courage of Faith," has been translated into many languages, and thousands of copies have been printed and distributed. This novena shows the value of courage and of self-surrender to our Lady in the shrine as an unchangeable attitude in his life. The Father Joseph Kentenich Secretariate deals with everything to do with his process of beatification and canonisation, which was officially opened in Treves on 10 February 1975.

Fr Kentenich is dead, but this does not mean that his mission has come to an end. In the mystery of the communion of saints he remains present in a new way in this world. The Second Vatican Council teaches that the union of those who are still on pilgrimage on earth with their brothers and sisters who have fallen asleep in the peace of Christ by no means ceases, but, according to the faith of the Church, is strengthened by the communion of spiritual goods (cf. Lumen Gentium 49). This was Fr Kentenich's belief when, on 8 December 1944 as a prisoner in Dachau, he said, "And if in his wise Providence God suddenly sends the angel of death to us to transplant us into another world in which he will reveal his plans to us, we hope that in close connection with all our loved ones we may be able to be and do more for Schoenstatt than while here on earth".

A prophet's mission includes a prophet's fate. In the normal course of events men with such a charism are not understood during their lifetime, because they are ahead of their times. Only after their death do people begin to discover and acknowledge them, and start to carry out their words. This is also a criterion by which one can distinguish between a true and a false prophet. And this is how it has to be, because a man of God who is motivated by the Holy Spirit does not try to force through his own plans, but the plans of God; his words do not come from himself, but God speaks through him. In the course of his most active life Fr Kentenich spoke countless prophetic words. I should like to recall here what he said on 18 October 1914 in the ancient chapel of St Michael in Schoenstatt: "I should like to make this place a place of pilgrimage, a place of grace... All who come here to pray should experience Mary's glories." After six decades we can see that his words have been fulfilled. The ancient chapel, at that time half abandoned, has been transformed into a place of pilgrimage and grace. Even more, since 1943 it has been multiplied through the daughter shrines, of which there are by now almost eighty throughout the world – in Madrid and in Sydney, in Milwaukee and Buenos Aires, in Guayaquil and Cape Town, in Santiago, Chile and in Lisbon.

Throughout his life Fr Kentenich bore witness to his faith in our Lady's great mission for the present-day world and its future. He not only saw her as our Mother and our Intercessor with the Triune God, but also her relatedness to man. He saw her as the great Victress over the anthropological heresies, that is, all the heresies in theory and practice about the evaluation of what, according to God's plan, goes to make up the identity and goal of mankind. He saw her as the great Educator, who, from the Schoenstatt shrines, wants to show in a special way that she is the educator of a new and truly free person (free from all that is contrary to the divine, and free for all that is divine). She is the Educator of both the élite and the masses; the great Victress over every diabolical influence, over every attack of the ''power of darkness''. He prophesied the coming of a new and exceptionally Marian era towards which the world and the Church are making their pilgrim way. (''We are approaching a time which will be so Marian in character that the world will not have seen its like before.'')

In the course of his hard life Fr Kentenich never stopped loving. He became a father who has hundreds, indeed thousands of sons and daughters. He knew how to remain joyful to the end – an indellible mark of the Holy Spirit on his life, a pledge of the resurrection and future glory. Fr Kentenich lives!

CHRONOLOGY

1885 18 November:	*Joseph Kentenich born at Gymnich near Cologne, Germany.*
19 November:	*Baptised in the parish church dedicated to St Kunibert.*
1910 8 July:	*Ordained a priest at the Pallottine Mission House at Limburg on the Lahn River.*
10 July:	*Celebrated his First Holy Mass.*
1912 October:	*Appointed Spiritual Director of the House of Studies at Schoenstatt.*
27 October:	*The first talk to the boys entitled "Programme", later known as the Pre-founding Document.*
1914 19 April:	*Foundation of the Marian Sodality from which the future Schoenstatt Movement developed.*
July:	*The Sodality is given the use of the ancient chapel of St Michael.*
1 August:	*The start of World War I.*
18 October:	*Foundation day of the Schoenstatt Movement.*
1916	*Incorporation of Vincent Pallotti's idea of the Apostolic World Federation as one of the essential goals of the Schoenstatt Movement. The foundation of the "outer organization". Publication of the first issue of the "MTA".*
1918 4 October:	*Josef Engling falls in battle near Cambrai, France.*

1919 18 July:	*Fr Kentenich is released from other duties and can dedicate himself to the growing Schoenstatt Movement.*
20 August:	*Foundation of the Apostolic Union at Hoerde.*
6 November:	*Letter from Fr Kentenich to the group leaders of the Union with directives for their future work.*
1920 20 August:	*Foundation of the Apostolic League.*
8 December:	*The start of the first group for women.*
1926 1 October:	*Official foundation of the Secular Institute of the Schoenstatt Sisters of Mary.*
1928 15 August:	*Blessing of the new Retreat House (Bundesheim) at Schoenstatt.*
1933	*National Socialism seizes power in Germany. The first sisters are sent to South Africa.*
1939 April:	*The House of Studies at Schoenstatt is requisitioned by the Nazis and becomes a teachers' training college.*
18 October:	*Letter from Fr Kentenich from Switzerland on the occasion of the twenty-fifth anniversary of Schoenstatt's foundation (Second Founding Document).*
10 December:	*Crowning of our Lady's picture in the original shrine.*

1941 20 September:	*Fr Kentenich is ordered to present himself at the Gestapo prison in Coblenz. He is questioned and detained. He spends four weeks in solitary confinement in the bunker.*
1942 20 January:	*Fr Kentenich decides not to make use of the possibility to avoid being sent to the concentration camp.*
11 March:	*He is transferred to the concentration camp at Dachau.*
13 March:	*Arrival at Dachau.*
16 July:	*Foundation of the Secular Institute of the Brothers of Mary and the Family Institute.*
1944 18 October:	*Third Founding Document. Foundation of the Schoenstatt International.*
1945 25 March:	*Schoenstatt is occupied by the American army.*
6 April:	*Fr Kentenich is released from concentration camp.*
20 May:	*Fr Kentenich returns to Schoenstatt.*
15 October:	*First October gathering in Schoenstatt.*
1946 2 February:	*Foundation of the Secular Institute of Our Lady of Schoenstatt.*
1947 14 March:	*Private audience with Pope Pius XII. The start of his first international journey (Brazil / Uruguay / Argentina / Chile). Return to Germany.*
29 December:	*Leaves for South Africa.*

1949 20 May:	*Blessing of the shrine at Bellavista, Chile.*
31 May:	*Start of the fight "against mechanistic thinking".*
1950 19 January:	*Arrives in Rome to take part in the beatification of Vincent Pallotti on 22 January.*
1951 15 August:	*Start of the Apostolic Visitation at Schoenstatt. Fr Kentenich is removed from office.*
22 October:	*Start of the exile. Fr Kentenich has to leave Germany. He first goes to Switzerland and from there to Rome.*
1952 20 January:	*Blessing of the shrine at Florencio Varela, Argentina.*
21 June:	*Leaves for Milwaukee where he is to spend the next thirteen years of his exile.*
1960 8 July:	*Golden Jubilee of ordination.*
1964 12 October:	*Pope Paul VI decrees the autonomy of the Schoenstatt Movement.*
18 October:	*The Schoenstatt Family celebrates the fiftieth anniversary of its foundation.*
1965 17 September:	*Fr Kentenich leaves for Rome.*
22 October:	*Pope Paul VI ratifies the decision of the Holy Office to reinstate Fr Kentenich.*

18 November: *Celebration of Fr Kentenich's eightieth birthday.*

22 December: *Private audience with Pope Paul VI.*

24 December: *Return to Schoenstatt after an absence of fourteen years.*

1967
16 July:
Visit to the concentration camp at Dachau to celebrate the twenty-fifth anniversary of the foundation of the Brothers of Mary and the Family Institute.

1968
9 June:
The Bishop of Treves consecrates the Church of the Blessed Trinity on Mount Schoenstatt.

7 September: *Letter to the Schoenstatt Family attending the 'Katholikentag' at Essen: With hope and joy, confident in the victory, we go with Mary into the post-modern era.*

15 September: *Death in the Adoration Church after he had celebrated Holy Mass there for the first time.*

20 September: *Funeral of Fr Joseph Kentenich. He was buried where he died. His tombstone is inscribed with the words "Dilexit Ecclesiam" – He loved the Church.*